The Pa

Anna Conrad

"Cook like a Caveman"
With special <u>Exercise Section</u> by
Dustin Mohr

Notice

This book is intended as a reference volume only, not as a medical manual. The information given here is designed to help you make informed decisions about your health. It is not intended as a substitute for any treatment that may have been prescribed by your doctor. If you suspect that you may have medical problems, we urge you to seek competent medical help.

Mention of specific companies, organizations, or authorities in this book does not imply endorsement by the publisher, nor does mention of specific companies, organizations or authorities imply that they endorse this book. Internet addresses and telephone numbers given in this book were accurate at the time it went to press.

This book may be purchased for business or promotional use or for special sales. For information, please email: chefanna@chefanna.net

Table of Contents

Why I Wrote This Book

Dustin Mohr, the author of the Exercise section in this book, introduced me to the Paleo diet. Dustin owns and operates "Mohr Fitness" in Johnson City, Tennessee. Dustin asked me to provide one Paleo recipe every day for 28 days to a select group of his clients for a 28 day Paleo challenge he conducted. Before I agreed, I researched the diet and determined whether or not I was comfortable with the approach. As with any diet I research and consider for promotion, I personally follow the diet for at least 2 weeks. Needless to say, I was very impressed with the Paleo diet.

Following are a few of the reasons why I chose to write this book:
1. The foods are extremely healthy
2. I was not hungry
3. I was very satisfied with the food
4. I lost 8 pounds
5. My blood pressure, heart rate and cholesterol stayed within healthy limits.

I agreed to provide recipes for Dustin's challenge. And I decided to provide prepared Paleo meals through my personal chef and catering business for the duration of the challenge. Today, the Paleo menu continues to be an offering at my business.

The Paleolithic Diet in Summary

The Paleo diet was first known as the Paleolithic diet and later shortened to Paleodiet or Paleo diet. Many refer to the diet as the caveman diet or the stoneage hunter-gatherer diet. The diet is named after the Paleolithic era, a period of time that lasted about 2.5 million years and ended about 10,000 years ago. It's widely believed the first humans lived during the Paleolithic period and derived their nutrition from a diet based on wild plants and animals. Today's interpretation of the Paleolithic diet consists mainly of meat, fish, vegetables, fruits, and nuts, and excludes grains, legumes, dairy products, salt, refined sugar, and processed oils.

The diet was first popularized in the 1970s by gastroenterologist Walter L. Voegtlin. Since that time the diet has been adapted by authors and researchers who have detailed the concept in several books and academic journals. There are a growing number of critics and proponents of the diet as it gains popularity in mainstream America and in particular in the athletic community.

When research this book I interviewed several medical professionals who believe that of the low carbohydrate diets to date, this diet has the most merit because it's roots are found in the earliest form of human beings before the agricultural, industrial and information ages tinkered with the food chain.

Proponents of Paleolithic nutrition base their beliefs on the premise that humans are genetically wired to best accept the diet of our Paleolithic ancestors and our genetics have scarcely changed since the Paleolithic era. A central argument for the diet is many diseases that humans suffer from today (and our Paleolithic ancestors did not) are categorized as "diseases of civilization". And assuming a diet that predates modern agricultural methods might rid humans of such diseases.

The Paleo dietary approach is often controversial with some anthropologists and nutritionists who argue it's a fad diet and the reason our Paleo ancestors did not suffer from diseases of civilization was due to a lack of calories in their diets vs. the composition of their diets. There is also some disagreement on the actual composition of the diet and the idea that one diet is right for every single human.

My recommendation is to review the foods list and if it looks like it might work for you, try it for 28 days. If at the end of 28 days, you are making positive progress toward your health goals and the diet agrees with you maybe you should consider continuing the diet longer term.

How Do I Go Paleo?

Okay you've read the "for" and "against" views of the diet and now you want to know how to get started with the diet. Read on!

Take an inventory of your refrigerator and freezer. Those items not on the encouraged foods list or foods to eat in moderation list get donated to a local food bank, no exceptions. If you keep them in the house you are likely to eat them. No, you shouldn't keep them for the kids. Remember if you think this diet is healthy for you and you shouldn't be eating chips and cookies, then it's true for your children too!

On Saturday or Sunday, choose from the recipes section which recipes you will make for the following week. Create a grocery list and go shopping. Make sure you eat before shopping so you aren't tempted to purchase something not on your approved foods list.

Food Do's and Don'ts

Exactly which items do and do not fit into the Paleo diet foods list is not always an easy answer to follow. In its purest form, the theory of the Paleo diet states that if your ancestors didn't eat it - you shouldn't either.

On the other hand, some foods that our ancestors did not eat are known to be very nutritious. For example, beans are a great source of numerous nutrients and dairy products can be a great source of calcium and protein. Some experts urge that a slightly less strict, slightly more modest form of the Paleo diet should be followed for optimal health. You will need to first decide *if* you should implement the Paleo diet, and then decide *how* to fit it in your own life.

Many of the recipes in this book use coconut fat because that's the cooking fat of choice for most Paleo dieters. But you can substitute any approved fat for the coconut fat in most recipes.

When approaching food for the Paleo diet think about them as you would approach a traffic signal; green, yellow and red light.

Green Light Foods: Foods that you may eat without restriction.

Yellow Light Foods: Foods you should approach with caution and consume in moderation.

Red Light Foods: Foods you should avoid because in all likelihood they were not available to our Paleo ancestors.

Green Light Foods

Certain foods are encouraged on the Paleo diet because they support the principles of the diet and closely match what our ancestors might have consumed. Boredom with food is one of the top reasons people abandon a diet. Eat a variety of meats, fish, poultry, eggs, vegetables, fruits and nuts and keep the diet interesting!

Lean Meats
Lean cuts of meat are a great way to get protein in your diet and keep you feeling full and satisfied. I prefer to eat meats from grassfed animals because that's what our ancestors would have eaten. Following are several examples of lean meats. But don't let this limit you, feel free to prepare lean meat of all kinds and use grassfed versions as often as possible for maximum benefits.

Lean meats commonly recognized as acceptable for the Paleo Diet because they would have been available to our Paleo ancestors:

Lean Beef (trimmed of fat):_flank steak, top sirloin steak, extra-lean hamburger (no more than 7% fat, extra fat drained off after cooking), London broil, chuck steak and lean veal.

Lean Pork (trimmed of visible fat): pork tenderloin & pork chops.

Rabbit meat (any cut)
Goat meat (any cut)

Organ meats
Organ meats are one of the most nutrient-dense foods available, rich with vitamins, minerals, amino acids, and other nutrients. Our ancestors knew the value of organ meats. For example let's look at the nutrients contained in beef kidneys.

Nutrients in 4 ounces raw beef kidney*:
Calories: 121, Protein: 18.7g, Carbohydrate: 2.45g, Total Fat: 3.5g, Fiber: 0.0g

*Excellent source of: Iron (8.3mg), Vitamin B12 (30.5mcg), Vitamin A (994 IU), and Folate (90.4mcg)

Organ meats commonly recognized as acceptable for the Paleo Diet because they would have been available to our Paleo ancestors:

Beef, lamb, pork, and chicken livers

Beef, pork, and lamb tongues
Beef, lamb, and pork marrow
Beef, lamb, and pork "sweetbreads"

Game meat

Whether you purchase them at the grocery store or hunt them like our ancestors did, game meats are a delicious and nutritious addition to your menu planning.

Following are commonly recognized as game meats acceptable for the paleo diet because they would have been available to our Paleo ancestors. But don't let this list stop you from considering other lean game meats.

Alligator, Bear, Bison (buffalo), Caribou, Elk, Emu, Goose, Kangaroo, Muscovy duck, New Zealand Cervena Deer, Ostrich, Quail, Rattlesnake, Reindeer, Squab, Turtle, Venison, and Wild boar, Wild Turkey

Poultry

Poultry meat is not only tasteful, easy to prepare and appropriate for different food combinations, but also a natural source of vitamins, minerals, proteins and healthy fats. Consider the following poultry when planning your Paleo Menu and use grassfed poultry when possible.

Lean poultry commonly recognized as acceptable for the Paleo Diet because they would have been available to our Paleo ancestors:

Lean Poutry (white meat, skin removed); Chicken breast, Turkey breast, Game hen breasts

Eggs
All natural, high-quality protein like that found in eggs is a great way to provide active adults and children with the energy needed on their busiest days.

Eggs commonly recognized as acceptable for the Paleo Diet because they would have been available to our Paleo ancestors:

Chicken, Duck, Goose

Fish & Shellfish
Eating the fish and shellfish, on our encouraged foods list, is an extremely efficient and healthy way to gain high-quality proteins with the right amount of amino acids needed for healthy body function. The fats in fish and shellfish are predominantly omega-3 fatty acids. And Fish oil is a natural source of vitamin D.

Fish commonly recognized as acceptable for the Paleo Diet because they would have been available to our Paleo ancestors:

Bass, Bluefish, Cod, Drum, Eel, Flatfish, Grouper, Haddock, Halibut, Herring, Mackerel, Monkfish, Mullet, Northern pike, Orange roughy, Perch, Red snapper, Rockfish, Salmon, Scrod, Shark, Striped bass, Sunfish, Tilapia, Trout, Tuna, Turbot, Walley, Any other commercially available fish

Shellfish commonly recognized as acceptable for the Paleo Diet because they would have been available to our Paleo ancestors:

Abalone, Clams, Crab, Crayfish, Lobster, Mussels, Oysters, Scallops, and Shrimp

Vegetables
Diets rich in vegetables help to lower blood pressure reduce the risk of heart disease and possibly some cancers, promote good eye health and digestive system health. Vegetables also help us control our blood sugar and, as a result, our appetite.

We should eat at least nine (about 4 ½ cups total) of Paleo encouraged vegetables and fruits each day. Choose a variety of types and colors. The darker green, red, orange or yellow the better.

Vegetables commonly recognized as acceptable for the Paleo Diet because they would have been available to our Paleo ancestors:

Artichokes, Asparagus, Beet greens, Beets, Bell peppers, Broccoli, Brussels sprouts, Cabbage, Carrots, Cauliflower, Celery, Collards, Cucumbers, Dandelions, Eggplant, Endives, Green onions, Kale, Kohlrabi, Lettuce, Mushrooms, Mustard greens, Onions, Parsley, Parsnips, Peppers (all kinds), Pumpkins, Purslane, Radishes, Rutabaga, Seaweed, Spinach, Squash (all kinds), Swiss chard, Rhubarb, Tomatillos, Tomatoes (actually a fruit, but most people think of it as a vegetable), Turnip greens, Turnips, and Watercress

Fruits

Fruits and vegetables can be great sources of the nutrients important for healthy bones, decreasing coronary heart disease, reduced brain and spinal cord defects, healthy blood and functioning of cells, healthy blood pressure, healthy teeth and gums, healing of cuts and wounds and healthy eyes and skin.

Fruits commonly recognized as acceptable for the Paleo Diet because they would have been available to our Paleo ancestors:

Apple, Apricot, Avocado, Banana, Blackberry, Blueberry, Boysenberry, Cantaloupe, Carambola, Cassava melon, Cherimoya, Cherry, Cranberry, Figs, Gooseberry, Grapefruit, Grape, Guava, Honeydew melon, Kiwi, Lemon**, Lime***,

Lychee, Mango, Nectarine, Orange, Papaya, Passion fruit, Peach, Pear, Persimmon, Pineapple, Plum, Pomegranate, Raspberry, Star fruit, Strawberry, Tangerine, Watermelon, and all other fruits

**Note: The juice of 1 lemon is approximately 1 Tbsp. The juice of 1 lime is approximately 1 Tbsp. You must use a fresh lemon or lime to get the juice.

Nuts and Seeds

Many nuts and seeds include the nutrients magnesium, manganese, protein, fiber, zinc and phosphorus.

Nuts are naturally cholesterol-free and only contain traces of sodium (raw nuts).

Nuts commonly recognized as acceptable for the Paleo Diet because they would have been available to our Paleo ancestors:

> Almonds, Cashews, Pecans, Hazelnuts and Filberts

<u>Yellow Light Foods</u>

The following foods are okay to eat in moderation but if you can minimize their use you will be best able to control your weight.

Oils & Fats
Consume a maximum of four tablespoons or less each day when your goal is to lose or maintain your weight.

Coconut Oil, Animal Tallow, Olive oil, and Avocado oil.

Poultry
Whole chicken, Whole turkey and Whole game hens

Fatty Meats our Paleo ancestors may have eaten these but their diet was calorically restricted and our diets are not. So there is not a need to consume lots of extra fat to get the necessary calories for energy needed each day.

Bacon (no artificial ingredients), Fatty beef roasts, Beef ribs, Fatty cuts of beef, Fatty ground beef, T-bone steaks, Poultry thighs, skin legs or wings, Fatty pork chops, Fatty pork roasts, Pork ribs, Pork sausage, Lamb chops, Lamb roasts, Leg of lamb

Nuts & Seeds (no more than 4 ounces per day)
Pine Nuts, Pumpkin Seeds, Sunflower Seeds, Brazil Nuts, Chestnuts, Macadamia Nuts, Pistachios (unsalted), Sesame Seeds, and Walnuts

Beverages

Diet Sodas, Beer (women - 12 ounces, men - 24 ounces), Coffee, Tea, Alcohol, neat (4 ounces per day), and Wine (women - 4 ounces, men - 8 ounces)

Dried fruits

No more than 2 ounces per day.

Red Light Foods

Dairy products commonly assumed not available for consumption by our Paleo ancestors:

All processed foods made with dairy products including: Powdered Milk, Ice cream, Butter, Cheese, Nonfat dairy creamer, Skim milk, Frozen yogurt, Ice milk, Whole milk, Yogurt, Cream, Dairy spreads, and Low-fat Milk

Cereal Grains commonly assumed not available for consumption by our Paleo ancestors:

Barley (barley soup, barley bread, & all processed foods made with barley), Corn (corn on the cob, corn tortillas, corn chips, cornstarch, corn syrup), Millet, Oats (steel-cut oats, rolled oats & all processed foods made with oats), Rice (brown rice, white rice, top ramen, rice noodles, basmati rice, rice cakes, rice flour, and all processed foods made with rice), Rye (rye bread, rye crackers, and all processed foods made with rye), Sorghum, Wheat (bread, rolls, muffins, noodles, crackers, cookies, cake, doughnuts, pancakes, waffles, pasta, spaghetti, lasagna, wheat tortillas, pizza, pita bread, flat bread, and all processed foods made with wheat or wheat flour), and Wild Rice

Cereal Grain-like Seeds commonly assumed not available for consumption by our Paleo ancestors:

Amaranth, Buckwheat, and Quinoa

Legumes commonly assumed not available for consumption by our Paleo ancestors:

All beans (Adzuki beans, Black beans, Broad beans, Fava beans, Field beans, Garbanzo beans, Horse beans, Kidney beans, Lima beans, Mung beans, Navy beans, Pinto beans, Red beans, String beans, White beans including Great Northern, Navy and Cannellini), Black-eyed peas, Chickpeas, Peanuts (and Peanut Butter), Lentils, Snowpeas, Peas, Sugar Snap Peas, Miso, Soybeans and all soybean products, including tofu

Starchy Vegetables commonly assumed not available for consumption by our Paleo ancestors:

Starchy tubers, Sweet potatoes, Cassava root, Yams, Tapioca pudding, Manioc, Potatoes and all potato products (French fries, potato chips, etc.)

Industrially processed, high sodium foods
commonly assumed not available for consumption
by our Paleo ancestors:

Bacon (containing ingredients), Processed Meats,
Pork rinds, Cheese, Salami, Deli Meats,
Frankfurters, Hot Dogs, Ketchup, Pickled foods,
Olives, Salted nuts, Salted spices, Sausages
(containing artificial ingredients), Smoked, dried
and salted fish or meat (containing artificial
ingredients), canned meats or fish.

Soft drinks and Fruit Juices commonly assumed
not available for consumption by our Paleo
ancestors:

All soft drinks, juices or beverages of any kind
sweetened with industrially processed sugars or
sweeteners

Sweets commonly assumed not available for
consumption by our Paleo ancestors:

Candy, industrially processed syrups, refined
sugars, industrially processed honey, industrially
processed sweeteners of any kind.

Twenty-Eight Day Challenge

Sometimes we need a little push to try something new. Challenge yourself to try the Paleo diet for twenty-eight days. To make it easier, we've included a twenty-eight day meal plan using recipes found in this book.

If you don't want to prepare a new recipe for each meal for 28 days, create a blank template (or use the ones provided beginning on page 212) like the one in this book, and create your own 28-day meal plan. Consider making an extra serving of the recipes and have for breakfast, lunch or dinner another day during the week.

Now what are you waiting for? Go Paleo!

28-Day Challenge Weeks 1 & 2 Menus

Day	Week 1	Week 2
Mon	B: Morning Smoothie L: Spicy Scallop Salad D: Chicken Masala	B: Veggies & Eggies L: Curried Shrimp & Spinach D: Asian Beef Heart Stir-Fry
Tue	B: Almost Flour Pancakes L: Grape & Broccoli Salad D: Spicy Pulled Pork	B: Morning Smoothie L: Irish Kidney Soup D: Nectarine & Onion Pork
Wed	B: Shrimp Avocado Omelet L: Creamy Mushroom Stew D: Basil & Chilies Beef Stir-Fry	B: Omelet Muffins L: Chicken & Zucchini Hot Salad D: Almond Crusted Salmon
Thu	B: Pumpkin Muffins L: Tossed Salad with Orange and Rosemary Vinaigrette D: Paleo Meatloaf	B: Almond Butter Oatmeal L: Waldorf Salad D: Barbecue Juneau Shrimp
Fri	B: Almond Butter Oatmeal L: Ratatouille D: Olive, Lemon & Garlic Chicken	B: Almond Flour Pancakes L: Bison Chili D: Paleo Pizza
Sat	B: Western Omelet L: Cilantro Turkey Burgers D: Lemon, Dill Trout	B: Morning Smoothie L: Simple Stuffed Portobello D: Butter Chicken
Sun	B: Morning Smoothie L: Chicken Fajitas D: Paleo Spaghetti	B: Carrot Banana Muffins L: Citrus Beef Salad Stir-Fry D: Hot Cilantro Shrimp

28-Day Challenge Weeks 3 & 4 Menus

Day	Week 3	Week 4
Mon	B: Morning Smoothie L: Baba-ghanoush D: Hungarian Beef Goulash	B: Veggies & Eggies L: Minted Pesto Chicken Stir-Fry D: Duck & Oranges Stir-Fry
Tue	B: Almost Flour Pancakes L: Salad w/Caesar Dressing D: Coconut Curry Stir-Fry	B: Morning Smoothie L: Spicy Shrimp Stir-Fry D: Cilantro Pork Stir-Fry
Wed	B: Shrimp Avocado Omelet L: Lemon & Garlic Scallops D: Spicy Chicken & Herb Sauce	B: Omelet Muffins L: Butternut Squash Soup D: Ginger Citrus Roast Chicken
Thu	B: Pumpkin Muffins L: Salmon w/Asparagus & Roasted Beets D: Steak & Eggs	B: Almond Butter Oatmeal L: Waldorf Salad D: Barbecue Juneau Shrimp
Fri	B: Almond Butter Oatmeal L: Cabbage & Apple Stir-Fry D: Liver & Onions	B: Almond Flour Pancakes L: Bison Chili D: Paleo Meatloaf
Sat	B: Western Omelet L: Cilantro Turkey Burgers D: White Wine & Garlic Mussels	B: Morning Smoothie L: Salad wi/Balsamic Vinaigrette D: Braised Oxtail
Sun	B: Morning Smoothie L: Tomato & Egg Stir-Fry D: Pork Tenderloin with Apples & Onions	B: Carrot Banana Muffins L: Vegetable Kabobs D: Salmon with Coconut Cream Sauce

Recipe Index

Breakfast Ideas

Lunches and Dinners

Miscellaneous

Recipes

Almond Flour Pancakes

<u>Serves 2</u>
Ingredients
1 cup almond flour
1/2 cup of apple sauce
1 Tbsp coconut flour
2 eggs
1/4 cup water (consider seltzer water for slightly fluffier pancakes)
1 Tbsp coconut oil
Cinnamon, to taste

Preparation

Combine all ingredients in a bowl. The batter will appear a little thicker than normal pancake mix.

Drop 1/4 cup of batter onto a lightly oiled, non-stick frying pan over medium heat. You might want to shape the pancakes with the scoop to keep them from being too thick.

Flip like a normal pancake when bubbles start showing up on the top.

Put on a plate and add berries.

Almond Butter Oatmeal

<u>Serves 1</u>

Ingredients

3 Tbsp organic unsweetened applesauce

1 Tbsp raw, chunky almond butter

1/2 Tbsp - 1 Tbsp of raw unsweetened coconut milk

Cinnamon to taste

Preparation

Combine all ingredients in a pot on the stove.

Add more coconut milk to thin out the consistency, if desired.

Heat on medium heat until desired temperature, stirring often. Or, microwave for about 45 seconds and stir.

Carrot Banana Muffins

<u>Serves 4-6</u>
Ingredients
2 cups blanched almond flour
2 tsp baking soda
1 tsp sea salt
1 Tbsp cinnamon
1 cup dates, pitted
3 ripe bananas
3 eggs
1 tsp apple cider vinegar
1/4 cup coconut oil
1 1/2 cups carrots, shredded
3/4 cup walnuts, finely chopped
Muffin paper liners

Preparation

In a small bowl, combine almond flour, baking soda, salt, and cinnamon.

In a food processor, combine dates, bananas, eggs, vinegar and oil and process until mostly smooth.

Transfer mixture to a large bowl.

Blend dry mixture into wet until thoroughly combined.

Fold in carrots and walnuts.

Spoon mixture into paper lined muffin tins.

Bake at 350° for 25 minutes or until a toothpick comes out clean when inserted in the center of a muffin.

Pumpkin Muffins

<u>Serves 4-6</u>

Ingredients
1 1/2 cups almond flour
3/4 cup canned pumpkin
3 large whole eggs
1 tsp baking powder
1 tsp baking soda
1/2 tsp ground cinnamon
1 1/2 tsp pumpkin pie spice
1/8 tsp salt
1 whole ripe mashed banana
2 tsp almond butter
5 whole almonds (or 1/8 cup sliced almonds)

Preparation

Grease 6 muffin tins with coconut oil (or use paper muffin cups and add about 1/2 tsp melted coconut oil to batter).

Mix all ingredients. Pour mix into the 6 tins.

Bake at 350 F for 25 minutes on the middle rack or until a toothpick comes out clean when inserted in the center of a muffin.

Stick almonds in the top when muffins come out of the oven.

Western Omelet

<u>Serves 2</u>

Ingredients

4 eggs

1 Tbsp Olive oil

1/3 cup chopped onion

1/3 cup chopped bell peppers

1/2 cup chopped tomato

1 cup spinach

4 oz diced lean meat of your choice

Sea salt and black pepper to taste

Preparation

Crack eggs into bowl and whisk.

Coat non-stick skillet with olive oil. Pour half of the eggs into a skillet. Cook over medium heat. Tilt pan and lift edges of omelet with a fork to allow runny egg to reach sides and cook.

Add half of the chopped vegetables andl lean meat to the one side of the eggs when the eggs have begun to set.

Using a spatula, fold the empty half of egg over top of the ham and vegetables. Cook for 1-2 minutes longer, and then serve.

Repeat the process with the remaining ingredients.

Omelet Muffins

<u>Serves 2</u>
Ingredients
6 eggs
1/4 to 1/2 cup cooked meat (your choice of lean meat) cut or crumbled into small pieces
1/2 cup diced vegetables (asparagus, peppers, and broccoli work well, but use whatever is on hand)
1/4 tsp salt
1/8 tsp ground pepper
1/8 cup mayonnaise (see recipe on page 167)
1/8 cup water

Preparation
Preheat oven to 350 degrees.

Grease 6 muffin tins with coconut oil or line with paper baking cups.

Beat the eggs in a medium bowl and add meat, vegetables, salt, ground pepper, and any other ingredients and stir to combine.

Pour mixture into the muffin cups. Bake for 18-20 minutes.

Cool for 5 minutes on a rack and remove from muffin pan. Serve warm. Refrigerate extra muffins for later and microwave them for 15-20 seconds to reheat.

Shrimp Avocado Omelet

<u>Serves 2</u>

Ingredients

1/2 ripe tomato, diced

1/2 ripe avocado, diced

1 Tbsp fresh cilantro, chopped (optional)

Sea salt and freshly ground black pepper, to taste (optional)

4 eggs, beaten

1 Tbsp olive oil

7 to 8 cooked shrimp, chopped

Preparation

Toss tomato, avocado, and cilantro together in a small bowl. Season to taste with salt and pepper. Set aside.

Beat eggs in a separate small bowl just until whites and yolks are combined, not long enough to become frothy.

Over medium-high heat, heat oil in an 8-inch skillet (preferably slope-sided and non-stick). Tilt skillet to spread oil evenly around and up sides. Pour eggs into the hot skillet, tilting and shaking the pan gently with one hand while stirring eggs briskly with the flat of a fork. Tilt pan and lift edges of omelet with a fork to allow runny egg to reach sides and cook.

When eggs just begin to set (no runny egg left), add shrimp pieces, spreading them over the center third of the omelet. Immediately use the fork to fold each side of omelet up over center filling. Tilt the pan to help roll omelet into a loose cylinder. Cook 10 to 30 seconds longer, depending on how brown you prefer the bottom (check for brownness by lifting a corner).

Slide omelet onto a warmed plate, top with tomato-avocado mixture and serve.

Veggies and Eggies

Serves 2

Ingredients

1/2 cup Kale, chopped

1/2 cup Chard, chopped

1/4 onion, diced

1 clove garlic, minced

1 1/2 Tbsp coconut oil

4 eggs

1 avocado, sliced and pitted

Preparation

Sauté kale, chard, onion, and garlic in coconut oil. Once everything softens up and the kale and chard reduce, transfer to a plate.

With the pan still hot, cook the eggs over easy in the leftover juices of the sauté.

When the eggs are cooked, layer them on top of the kale/chard mixture. Top with the sliced avocado.

Chopped Mushrooms, Eggs and Onions

<u>Serves 5-6</u>

Ingredients

1 medium onion, finely diced

1/4 cup coconut oil

10 to 12 medium white mushrooms, finely chopped

8 hard-boiled eggs, peeled and finely chopped

Freshly ground black pepper, to taste

Preparation

Sauté onion in the coconut oil until golden brown. Add the mushrooms and sauté another 5-6 minutes, stirring frequently, until mushrooms are softened and turned dark.

Remove sauté from heat and let cool. Mix together with the eggs and pepper.

Chill until ready to serve.

Morning Smoothie

Start with a base of coconut milk, I usually use a whole can. Add plenty of any fruit you'd like. I like to use frozen berries. I use mixed berries, strawberries, blackberries or even cranberries, which give a very tangy taste. The berries add lots of great color to the smoothie and provide plenty of beneficial antioxidants. Add one or two whole raw eggs for extra protein and fat. Optionally add one or two spoonfuls of your favorite nut butter. The taste will be really subtle in your final smoothie, but it will still be there as a nice aftertaste.

I also like to put in a good dose of pure vanilla extract to finish this flavor explosion.

Lunches and Dinners

Creamy Mushroom Stew

Serves 4

Ingredients

1 lb of mixed mushrooms, chopped, with tough
portion of stems removed (Portobello and White
Button are a great combination)
1/4 cup of coconut oil
2 onions, chopped
4 cloves garlic, minced
Handful of fresh thyme, leaves picked
1/4 cup or so of red wine or beef stock (see recipe
on page 195)
1/2 cup full-fat coconut milk
2 green onions, chopped
Sea salt and freshly ground black pepper to taste

Preparation

Before chopping the mushrooms, rinse them to

remove any excess dirt and then pat dry.

Heat a large skillet over medium heat. Add the coconut oil.

Stir in the onions and garlic. Cook until they begin to brown, about 7 minutes.

Add the mushrooms and season to taste with sea salt and freshly ground black pepper. Cook until moisture from mushrooms evaporates.

Add the stock and coconut milk and stir well to ensure that the flavors are dispersed evenly.

Once the stew has simmered for a few minutes, add in the thyme leaves, green onions and adjust the salt and pepper seasoning. Heat over low heat for a few more minutes so that it thickens.

Serve warm.

Irish Kidney Soup

<u>Serves 8</u>

Ingredients

1 1/2 lbs lamb kidneys or lamb leg

2 onions, coarsely chopped

2 carrots, sliced

1 1/2 Tbsp lemon juice

10 whole black peppercorns

2 large sprigs thyme

1 bay leaf

8 cups beef or lamb stock (see recipe on page 195)

2 Tbsp coconut oil

Sea salt and freshly ground black pepper to taste

Preparation

Prepare the kidneys by removing any membrane covering them, if present. Cut them in half lengthwise and cut around the fatty white core to remove it. Cut each kidney half into 1/2 inch slices.

Heat a stockpot over a medium heat, add the cooking fat and cook the onions, stirring occasionally, until they start to soften, about 6 minutes.

Add the kidney slices to the hot pot and brown them on each side.

Pour in the stock and add the whole peppercorns, thyme sprigs and bay leaf.

Bring to a boil, and then reduce to a simmer and cook, covered, for about 3 hours.

Add the carrot slices in the last 45 minutes of cooking.

When the soup is ready, discard the thyme sprigs, the bay leaf and use a slotted spoon to remove most of the whole peppercorns.

Add 1 or 2 Tbsp lemon juice, to taste, and serve.

Spicy Scallop Salad

<u>Serves 4</u>
Ingredients
1 red bell pepper, seeded and cut into strips
1 avocado, peeled, pitted and cubed
1 clove garlic, minced
2 tsp freshly ground black pepper
2 tsp cayenne pepper
1 tsp sea salt
1 lb small sea or bay scallops
3 Tbsp lemon juice (about 1.5 lemons)
1 Tbsp Paleo Mayonnaise, optional (see recipe on page 167)
Pinch of cayenne pepper
1 tsp Dijon or Paleo mustard (see recipe on page 178 & 180)
1/2 cup olive oil
2 big handfuls of mixed greens
Sea salt and freshly ground black pepper to taste
3 Tbsp coconut oil

Preparation

Complete all chopping first, saving the scallops for last to ensure they will be warm upon serving. Combine mixed greens, peppers and avocado in a large bowl and set aside.

In a small bowl, prepare the vinaigrette by whisking together the lemon juice, mayonnaise, and mustard. Once combined, slowly mix in the olive oil.

In a bowl large enough to hold the scallops, mix the cayenne, salt and pepper. Rinse the scallops and lightly pat dry.
Add the scallops to the spice mixture prepared in step 4 and ensure that they are evenly coated. Over medium heat, heat a skillet and melt the cooking fat in preparation for searing the scallops.

Your skillet must be hot prior to adding the scallops; however, do not allow the cooking fat to burn.

Place the scallops in the pan and cook for about 1-2 minutes per side, until they are opaque white and just cooked through.

Add the scallops to the bowl of mixed greens and veggies, and add the dressing over top. Serve while the scallops are still warm.

Chicken Masala

<u>Serves 4</u>
Ingredients
2 lbs skinless, boneless chicken thighs, cut into 1-inch pieces
1 cup full-fat coconut milk
1 onion, finely chopped
1/4 cup lemon juice
1/2 cup water or chicken stock (see recipe on page 195)
4 garlic cloves, minced
2 cups fresh cilantro leaves
1 cup fresh mint leaves
1 jalapeño pepper, chopped coarsely
1 1/2 tsp turmeric
1/2 tsp cinnamon
1/2 tsp ground cardamom
1/8 tsp ground cloves
3 Tbsp coconut oil
Sea salt and freshly ground black pepper to taste

Preparation

Heat a large skillet over medium heat and add the onion with the cooking fat. Cook, stirring occasionally, for about 5 minutes, or until the onion starts to soften. Add the chicken thighs as well as the turmeric to the skillet and continue cooking, while stirring occasionally, for about 7 minutes.

Meanwhile, place the lemon juice, water or stock, cilantro, mint, jalapeño and garlic in a blender or food processor and process to obtain a smooth purée.

After the chicken has cooked for about 7 minutes, add the cloves, cardamom and cinnamon. Cook for another minute. Pour in the coconut milk, season to taste with sea salt and freshly ground black pepper and add the herb purée. Bring to a simmer and let cook for about 15 minutes, until the chicken is well cooked and tender.

Nectarine & Onion Pork Tenderloin

Serves 6
Ingredients
6 Pork tenderloin, 6 ounces each, 1 inch thick,
trimmed of fat and silverskin.
3 nectarines, quartered
1 large onion, quartered
2 tsp Dijon or Paleo mustard (see recipe on page
178 & 180)
1 1/2 Tbsp lemon juice
1/4 cup fresh mint, coarsely chopped
2 Tbsp cooking fat + extra for rubbing the chops,
melted (see page 200)
Sea salt and freshly ground black pepper to taste

Preparation

Combine the nectarine and onion quarters in a
bowl along with the 2 Tbsp cooking fat and season
the mixture to taste with sea salt and freshly
ground black pepper.

Heat a skillet over medium heat; add the nectarine and onion mixture and cook, stirring frequently, until the nectarine quarters have softened, about 8 minutes. Set the cooked mixture aside to cool in a bowl. Wipe the skillet clean to cook the pork tenderloins.

Rub some additional cooking fat over the pork tenderloin on both sides and season them to taste with salt and pepper. Reheat the skillet over medium heat until hot. Add the pork tenderloin to the hot skillet and cook for about 3 minutes per side, until well cooked.

While the pork tenderloins are cooking, cut the cooked nectarine and onion quarters into 1/4 inch thick slices. Add the slices back to the bowl with their juices. Add the lemon juice, mustard and chopped mint to the nectarine and onion preparation and season to taste with salt and pepper.

Serve the cooked pork tenderloins topped with a generous portion of the nectarine and onion preparation.

Spicy Pulled Pork

<u>Serves 8-10</u>

Pulled pork ingredients

1 pork shoulder or butt roast, about 5-6 lbs

3 Tbsp smoked paprika

1 Tbsp garlic powder

1 Tbsp dry mustard

3 Tbsp sea salt

Spicy sauce ingredients

1 1/2 cups apple cider vinegar

1/2 cup Paleo ketchup (see recipe on page 176 and 177)

1 cup Dijon or Paleo mustard (see recipe on page 178 & 180)

2 garlic cloves, minced

1 tsp cayenne pepper

1 tsp sea salt

1/2 tsp freshly ground black pepper

Preparation

Prepare the dry rub by combining the paprika, garlic powder, dry mustard and sea salt in a bowl.

Rub the pork all over with the spice rub and place in the refrigerator for a minimum of 1 but no more than 4 hours for the flavors to penetrate the meat. Preheat your oven to 300 F.

Place the marinated pork in the oven in a baking pan and bake for about 6 hours, until the meat is almost falling apart and is very tender.

While the pork is cooking, prepare the sauce by combining the vinegar, ketchup, mustard, garlic, cayenne pepper, salt and pepper in a small saucepan. Gently simmer, stirring occasionally, and simmer for about 10 minutes. When the pork is cooked, remove it from oven and let it rest for 10 minutes.

Pull the meat apart from the roast with two forks and place the meat shreds in a bowl.

Combine the spicy sauce with the pulled pork and serve the delicious and tender meat with your favorite side of salad.

Curried Shrimp and Spinach

<u>Serves 4</u>
Ingredients
2 lbs shrimp, peeled and deveined
2 Tbsp coconut oil
1 onion, chopped
2 tsp curry powder
2 tsp tomato paste
1/2 cup chicken stock (see recipe on page 195)
1 cup full-fat coconut milk
2 tightly packed cups shredded spinach
Sea salt and freshly ground black pepper to taste

Preparation

Heat a large skillet over medium-low heat and cook the onion in coconut oil until it begins to soften, about 3 minutes.

Season to taste with sea salt and freshly ground black pepper, stir in the curry powder and continue cooking for about one minute.

Place mixture in a blender or a food processor, add the tomato paste as well as the chicken stock and coconut milk. Process or blend until smooth.

Pour the mixture back in the skillet and bring to a simmer.

Add the shrimp and spinach. Cook, covered, for 3-5 minutes, until the shrimp are pink. Do not overcook or shrimp will become tough.

Spicy Chicken with Herb Sauce Recipe

Serves 4

Ingredients for chicken

4 boneless chicken breasts

2 Tbsp smoked paprika

2 tsp ground cumin

2 tsp ground mustard

2 tsp ground fennel seeds

1 tsp freshly ground black pepper

2 tsp sea salt

Coconut oil or tallow sufficient for frying

Ingredients for herb sauce

1 cup extra-virgin olive oil

2 cups fresh mint leaves

1 cup fresh flat-leaf parsley leaves

6 garlic cloves, roughly chopped

2 Tbsp homemade or Dijon mustard

1 green chili, seeded and chopped, optional

Sea salt and freshly ground black pepper to taste

Preparation

To prepare the sauce, place the mint, parsley, garlic and chili (optional), in the bowl of a food processor and process to chop roughly. Add the mustard, season to taste with salt and pepper and process again to combine. Slowly drizzle the olive oil in while the food processor is on, to create an emulsion. An emulsion is formed when all ingredients are in solution and do not separate when standing for a few moments.

To make the spice rub, combine the paprika, cumin, mustard powder, fennel, salt and pepper in a bowl. Rub the chicken breasts all over with cooking fat and sprinkle both sides with the spice mixture. Heat a frying pan over medium high heat, place fat in the pan and cook the chicken breasts for 3-5 minutes per side, or until internal temperature reads 160-165 F.

Serve the spicy chicken topped with the fresh herb sauce.

Steak and Eggs

<u>Serves 1</u>
Ingredients
1 good quality large steak (filet, sirloin, ribeye)
3 Tbsp of coconut oil or your favorite cooking fat
(tallow is excellent here)
2 free range eggs
Paprika to taste
Salt and pepper to taste

Preparation
Heat a pan over medium-high heat and add 2 Tbsp
of your chosen cooking fat.

Season steak with sea salt and freshly ground black
pepper and add to the hot pan. Cook the steak to
desired doneness; about 3 minutes on each side for
a medium rare steak or about 5 minutes per side
for medium.

Remove the steak from the pan, set aside and lower the temperature to medium-low. Add the rest of the cooking fat.

Crack eggs in the hot pan, season to taste with some paprika, salt and pepper, cover and cook until the whites are just set.

Serve the steak with the eggs on top.

Chicken Fajitas

<u>Serves 6</u>
Ingredients
3 pounds chicken breast, cut in thin strips
3 bell peppers
3 onions, sliced
2 Tbsp oregano, chili powder, cumin and coriander
6 chopped garlic cloves
Juice of 5 lemons
4 Tbsp cooking fat (coconut oil or tallow are excellent here)
Romaine or Butter Lettuce leaves to serve as "Tortilla"
Your choice of toppings: diced tomatoes, fermented pickles, sauerkraut, sliced avocados, salsa, guacamole (recipe on page 171), Paleo mayonnaise (recipe on page 168), or salsa verde (recipe on page 173).

Preparation

Combine chicken, bell peppers, onions, spices, garlic and lemon juice in a bowl and mix well. If preparing ahead of time, marinate in the refrigerator for up to 4 hours.

When ready to cook, heat a large skillet over medium heat. Cook the entire preparation with the cooking fat until the chicken is cooked through and the onion and bell pepper are soft.

Put the hot chicken preparation in a large bowl and let the people prepare their own fajitas on top of lettuce leaves with their favorite toppings.

Liver & Onions

<u>Serves 5</u>

Ingredients

4 large slices pork or beef liver

5 large onions, sliced

6 Tbsp lard or coconut oil

Salt and pepper to taste

Preparation

Heat a large skillet over medium-low heat and add 5 Tbsp of the cooking fat and the sliced onions. Cook slowly, stirring often, for about 20 to 25 minutes, until the onions are really soft and caramelized.

When onions are nearly done, heat another pan over a medium-high heat, add rest of the cooking fat and cook the liver, about 3 minutes on each side.

Serve the liver topped with the delicious and creamy cooked onions. This is also delicious served with a little bit of homemade salsa verde (recipe on page 173) on the side.

Baked Salmon with Asparagus & Roasted Beets

Serves 4
Ingredients
4 fresh wild salmon fillets
4 Tbsp coconut oil
4 tsp chopped dill
16 stalks of fresh asparagus, hard bases removed
4 medium red beets, cut in cubes
Salt and pepper to taste

Preparation

Preheat oven to 500 F.

Tear off four pieces of foil each large enough to wrap one fillet. Make a bed of beet cubes along with 4 stalks of asparagus on each of the four pieces of foil and place a fillet atop of foil and place a salmon fillet on the beds of vegetables.

Add 1 Tbsp of cooking fat and 1 tsp dill on top of each fillet and close the foil to form a little pocket. Bake in hot oven for about 10 minutes for each inch of thickness of the fish.

Make sure to check on the fish so it doesn't get overcooked. Fish is done when it flakes easily with a fork.

Serve topped with some more of your favorite fresh herbs. More dill is perfect, but cilantro is also really good.

Chicken & Zucchini Hot Salad

<u>Serves 4</u>

Ingredients

2 1/2 lbs chicken breast, cut into cubes

5 zucchini, cut into cubes

3 Tbsp coconut oil

1 Tbsp oregano

1 large onion, chopped

7 Tbsp Paleo mayonnaise (recipe on page 168)

Juice of 2 lemons

2 cloves garlic, minced very finely

1 head romaine lettuce, washed and shredded

Salt and pepper to taste

1/4 cup raw almonds, sliced, for topping

Preparation

Heat a large pan over a medium-high heat and cook the chicken cubes until done, about 8-10 minutes. Set aside.

In the same pan, with the rest of the cooking fat, add the onion and cook until soft, about 5 minutes. Add the zucchini cubes and oregano and season with salt and pepper. Cook until the zucchini cubes are soft, about 2-3 minutes.

In a bowl, mix the mayonnaise, lemon juice and garlic.

Add the hot cooked chicken, onion and zucchini to the mayonnaise preparation and mix well.

Add the romaine lettuce, mix well and serve in bowls. This hot salad is delicious topped with almonds.

Canned Salmon Salad

Serves 3
Ingredients
2 cans wild caught salmon
2 diced cucumbers, (peeling is optional)
1 chopped onion
1 large diced tomato
1 diced avocado
5-6 Tbsp extra virgin olive oil
Juice of 2 lemons
2 Tbsp chopped fresh dill, optional
Lettuce leaves for serving

Preparation

Drain liquid from the canned salmon and place in a bowl. Shred well with a fork.

Add the lemon juice and olive oil and mix well into the salmon.

Add the cucumbers, onion, tomato and avocado and mix again.

Add the dill, if using, season with salt and pepper and serve the cold salad over lettuce leaves.

Grape and Broccoli Salad

<u>Serves 6</u>

Ingredients

2 or 3 heads of broccoli, depending on their size

1 1/2 cup red or green grapes, halved

1/2 chopped onion

1/2 cup slivered or chopped almonds

1 1/4 cup Paleo mayonnaise (see recipe on page 168) or coconut milk

1/4 cup lemon juice

Preparation

Cut the broccoli in small florets. You can use the stalks as well, making sure to cut it in pieces about the same size as the florets.

Mix the florets with the almonds, chopped onion and halved grapes.

In a separate bowl, mix the mayonnaise with the lemon juice.

Add the dressing with the salad, mix well, and serve.

White Wine & Garlic Mussels

<u>Serves 4</u>

Buy mussels same day as serving. Plunge them in cold water, wash them, remove the beard (a stringy-like membrane attached to most of them) and discard any that are opened, even if only slightly. The opened ones are dead and the closed ones are still living. Don't worry if you have to discard several; that's normal.

Ingredients

4 lbs fresh mussels
2 cups white wine or chicken stock (see recipe on page 195)
2 chopped onions
5 finely chopped cloves garlic
1/3 cup of your favorite chopped fresh herbs (parsley and basil are excellent)
6 Tbsp coconut oil

Preparation

Wash, remove the beards and discard any of the opened mussels prior to cooking.

In a stockpot, combine the wine or stock, onions and garlic, bring to a boil and simmer for about 5 minutes.

Add the mussels to the pot, cover and increase the heat to medium-high so the sauce boils and creates steam that will cook the mussels.

When all the mussels have opened, add the herbs and cooking fat and remove from heat.

Serve in bowls with the white wine and garlic sauce.

Pork Tenderloin with Apples and Onions

<u>Serves 4</u>

Ingredients

4 pork tenderloins, 6 ounces each, 1-inch thick, fat
and silverskin trimmed.
3 Tbsp lard or coconut oil
2 large onion, sliced
4 sliced and cored apples
Salt and pepper to taste

Preparation

Heat a large pan over a medium-high heat. Season
the pork tenderloins with salt and pepper to taste.

Melt 2 Tbsp of the cooking fat and fry the chops,
about 5 minutes on each side, until well cooked
and browned.

Set the pork tenderloins aside, reduce the heat to medium-low, add the other tablespoon of cooking fat and add the onion and apple slices

Cook for about 4 minutes, until the onions have caramelized and the apple slices are slightly soft. Serve the chops with the topping of apple and onions.

Ratatouille

<u>Serves 8</u>

Ingredients

Up to 1 1/4 cup lard or olive oil

4 large tomatoes (plum tomatoes are best, but any kind will do)

2 lbs eggplants, cut in 1 inch cubes

2 large onions, sliced thinly

3 bell peppers of assorted colors, cut into 1 inch cubes

4 zucchinis, cut into 3/4 inch cubes

9 garlic cloves

1 cup chopped parsley

20 basil leaves, cut in half

Freshly ground black pepper and sea salt

Preparation

Remove the skin from the tomatoes if using fresh tomatoes. To do so: score an X on the bottom of each one and blanch them in boiling water for a minute. Remove them from the boiling water and transfer them to a bowl of cold water. When cold enough to handle, gently remove the skin starting where you scored them.

Chop the tomatoes and put them in a large pot with 1/3 cup of oil or fat with the parsley, basil and garlic. Cover the pot partially and simmer while stirring periodically for 30 minutes, or until the tomatoes are well broken down.

While the tomatoes are simmering, sprinkle sea salt on the eggplant cubes and put them in a colander in the kitchen sink. This step helps remove some of the moisture in the eggplants. Leave them in the colander while the tomatoes are simmering.

In a small skillet over medium heat, cook the onions in 3 Tbsp of the oil or fat for about 10 minutes with some sea salt still while the tomatoes are simmering.

Remove the onions with a slotted spoon, set aside and cook the bell peppers in the same manner with a little more oil or fat.

Remove the bell peppers with a slotted spoon, put them with the onions and repeat the process with the zucchini, but only for 6 minutes this time. Remove zucchini and set aside with the other vegetables. Pat the eggplants dry and repeat the process, cooking them for about 7 minutes, again adding some oil or fat.

Once the tomato preparation has simmered on its own long enough, add the previously cooked vegetables, season generously with sea salt and black pepper, cover and simmer for about another hour, until all the vegetables are very soft.

Serve hot, warm or cold, with a bit of extra basil or chopped parsley on top, if desired.

Olive, Garlic & Lemon Chicken

Serves 4

Ingredients

1/4 cup tallow, coconut oil or poultry fat

1/2 lb Kalamata olives (black), cut in half

8 chicken thighs, with bones and skin

3 cups onions, sliced thin

30 gloves garlic, minced and smashed almost to a paste;

1/2 cup lemon juice

2 extra lemons, thickly sliced (remove seeds with the tip of a knife)

1 1/2 cups chicken stock (see recipe on page 195)

One bunch of picked thyme leaves or 1 teaspoon dried

Sea salt and freshly ground black pepper to taste

Preparation

Preheat oven to 350 F.

Melt the first 1/4 cup fat in a large ovenable pan over medium-high heat and brown the chicken pieces on all sides. Cook about 6 minutes total. Set the chicken aside.

Cook the onions until soft, about 3 minutes, and make sure to scrape all the chicken bits off the pan while doing so.

Add the garlic and cook for about 1 minute, until fragrant. Season with salt and pepper at this point. Add the chicken stock, thyme and lemon juice and return the chicken thighs to the pan, skin side up. Bring to a simmer and put the pan, covered, in the hot oven for about 20 minutes.

Remove the lid, add the halved olives as well as the lemon slices and bake for another 15 to 20 minutes uncovered. Serve the chicken with the olive, garlic and lemon sauce as well as lemon slices.

Tomato and Egg Stir-fry

<u>Serves 3</u>
Ingredients
1 Tbsp Coconut oil or favorite cooking fat
6 eggs
4 firm but ripe tomatoes, sliced in wedges
2 green onion, thinly sliced

Preparation
Whisk the eggs in a bowl and stir-fry in a hot wok with some cooking fat for a minute.

Thoroughly remove the stir-fried eggs from the wok with a spatula, reheat the wok and stir-fry the tomatoes for 2 minutes with more cooking fat. Return the eggs to the wok, add the green onions and stir-fry for another 30 seconds while mixing everything well. Serve while hot.

Coconut Curry Stir-fry

<u>Serves 2-3</u>

Ingredients

1 Tbsp Coconut oil

1 lb skinless chicken breast cut in thin slices

2 cups broccoli

1 can coconut milk

1 1/2 tsp curry powder

1 tsp grated ginger

A good bunch of fresh spinach - about 3 fistfuls

1/8 cup coconut flakes (optional)

Preparation

Prepare the sauce by mixing together the coconut milk, curry powder and grated ginger. Set aside. Stir-fry the chicken in a hot wok or large non-stick skillet. Remove the chicken from the wok, set aside.

Reheat the wok and stir-fry the onion with more cooking fat for about 2 minutes. Add the broccoli and stir-fry another 3 minutes.

Return the chicken to the wok, add the coconut curry sauce and the spinach and cook until the spinach is just wilted and the whole preparation is hot. Garnish with coconut flakes (optional).

Asian Beef Heart Stir-fry

<u>Serves 2</u>

Ingredients

1 Tbsp Coconut oil or your favorite cooking fat, tallow is perfect here

1 beef heart (about 1 lb)

1 1/2 cups green or yellow zucchini

1 tsp grated ginger

Juice of 1 lime

Fresh cayenne pepper to taste

Thinly sliced chili for garnishing

Preparation

Cut the beef heart into bite-sized cubes after having removed the fat and connective tissues. Heat wok over medium-high heat and stir-fry the heart in cooking for 3-5 minutes, depending upon desired doneness.

Remove the heart from the wok and set aside. Reheat the wok and stir-fry the zucchini with more fat for about 1 minute. Add the ginger, lime juice, cayenne pepper and return the heart cubes to the wok. Stir-fry for another minute to blend all the flavors together and bring out the flavors of the ginger and cayenne pepper.

Serve garnished with sliced chili.

Cabbage & Apple Stir-fry

<u>Serves 4-6</u>

Ingredients

1-2 Tbsp coconut oil

1 1/2 lb cabbage (a mix of red and green is ideal)

1 large apple

1 thinly sliced onion

1 finely chopped red chili

1 Tbsp chopped thyme

1 Tbsp apple cider vinegar

2/3 cup chopped almonds

Preparation

Chop cabbage finely and dry with a towel. Core and slice the apple.

Stir-fry the apple for 1 minute in coconut oil until it just barely starts to soften. Remove the apple from the wok and set aside.

Reheat the wok and stir-fry the onion for another minute with a little bit more cooking fat. Add the cabbage and stir-fry for another 3 minutes.

Return the apple slices, add the thyme and cider vinegar and cover to steam for a minute. Add the almonds and stir well. Serve.

Duck and Oranges Stir-Fry

Serves 2-3

Substitute chicken for the duck for a variation on the recipe. Bok choy works well with this dish, but any green leafy vegetable will work.

Ingredients

1 Tbsp coconut oil
1 roasted duck (3-5 lbs)
1 sliced onion
2 cloves garlic, minced
2 tsp grated ginger
1 Tbsp orange zest
2/3 cup orange juice
1/4 cup chicken stock (see recipe on page 195)
3 lbs bok choy leaves
1 segmented orange

Preparation

Pick the meat from the roasted duck and cut the skin in thin slices for garnish at the end.

Stir-fry the onion for 3 minutes with some cooking fat. Add ginger and garlic and stir-fry for 1-2 minutes. Add the orange juice, zest and stock and bring to a boil. Add the duck to the wok and let the whole preparation simmer for about 3 minutes.

Remove the meat from the wok, add the bok choy and cook until just wilted. Serve the duck on a bed of bok choy and garnish with orange segments and crispy duck skin.

Minted Pesto Chicken Stir-fry

<u>Serves 2-3</u>
Ingredients
1 Tbsp coconut oil
2 cups mint leaves
1/4 cup pine nuts
1/2 cup Parmesan, optional
1/4 cup olive oil
1 lb tender chicken, cut in thin strips
1 sliced onion
1 lb mushrooms of any kind, in smallish chunks

Preparation
Process the mint, pine nuts and Parmesan, if using, in a food processor and slowly add olive oil until well combined.

Heat the wok and stir-fry the chicken with your chosen fat. Remove the chicken from the wok and set aside.

Reheat wok and stir-fry the onion for 3-4 minutes. Add the mushrooms and stir-fry for another 2 minutes.

Return the chicken to the wok and stir in the mint pesto. Cook for another 3 minutes until everything is hot and serve.

Cilantro Pork Stir-fry

<u>Serves 2-3</u>

Ingredients

1 Tbsp coconut oil

1 lb tender pork, thinly sliced

4 finely chopped garlic cloves

1 Tbsp finely chopped ginger

1 cup cilantro leaves, chopped, divided

1/4 cup olive oil

2 onions, thinly sliced

1 red or green bell pepper, thinly sliced

1 Tbsp lime juice

Preparation

Mix the garlic, ginger, half the cilantro and all the olive oil in a bowl, add the pork and put in the refrigerator to marinate for 1-2 hours.

Heat your wok over medium-high heat and stir-fry the pork. Remove the pork and keep warm.

Return wok to heat and add more cooking fat and the onions. Stir-fry the onions for about 3 minutes. Add the bell pepper and stir-fry for another 3 minutes, until soft.

Return the pork to the wok with the lime juice and the other half of the cilantro leaves and cook for another minute while tossing to blend the flavors.

Basil and Chilies Beef Stir-fry

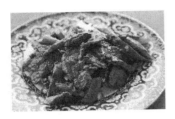

<u>Serves 2-3</u>
Ingredients
1 Tbsp coconut oil
3 finely chopped red chilies
3 minced garlic cloves
2 Tbsp water
1 lb tender beef, cut in thin slices
12 chopped asparagus spears
1 cup fresh basil leaves
Thinly sliced red chili for garnishing

Preparation
Mix the chopped chilies, garlic and water in a bowl and add the beef. Put in the refrigerator to marinate for about 2 hours.

Heat some fat in the wok, stir-fry the beef until done, about 3-5 minutes, remove and keep warm.

Return wok to heat, add more fat and stir-fry the asparagus about 2 minutes. Add 1/4-cup water or stock when the asparagus is almost cooked.

Return the beef to the wok, add the basil and cook for another minute. Garnish the finished dish with slices of chili.

Citrus Beef Salad Stir-fry

<u>Serves 2-3</u>

Ingredients

2 Tbsp coconut oil or tallow, divided

1 lb tender beef cut into thin strips

1 sliced onion

2 minced garlic cloves

1 tsp grated ginger

1 tsp lemon zest

1 tsp orange zest

1 Tbsp lemon juice

1 Tbsp orange juice

2 fists full of fresh spinach

1 lemon, segmented

1 orange, segmented

Preparation

Heat half of the fat in the wok, stir-fry the beef until done, about 3-5 minutes, remove and keep warm.

Make sure the wok regains its temperature, add the remaining cooking fat and stir-fry the onion, ginger and garlic for about 3 minutes.

Return the beef to the wok and add the orange and lemon juice. Bring to a boil and add the spinach a handful at a time. Cook until just wilted. Serve on a bed of segmented lemons and oranges.

Spicy Shrimp Stir-fry

Serves 3

Ingredients

2 Tbsp coconut oil

1 finely chopped small onion

1/2 cup olive oil

1 Tbsp lemon zest

3 cloves garlic, minced

1/2 cup lemon juice

2 small red chilies, seeded and finely chopped

1 Tbsp grated ginger

1 tsp turmeric

20-24 raw shrimp; shelled, deveined and rinsed

Preparation

Mix all ingredients except the shrimp and coconut oil together in a bowl; add the shrimp and cover. Marinate overnight.

When ready to cook, heat the coconut oil over medium-high heat, until shimmering hot, remove shrimp from marinade and stir-fry them until pink. Turn shrimp over at least once. Total cooking time is about 1-2 minutes. Remove shrimp to a bowl and keep warm.

Add the marinade to the wok and bring to a boil while stirring. Boil about 1-2 minutes, pour over shrimp and serve.

Lemon and Garlic Scallops

<u>Serves 6</u>

Ingredients

3 Tbsp garlic, minced

2 Tbsp lemon juice

3/4 cup coconut oil

2 lbs large scallops

Salt and pepper to taste

Fresh parsley or chives for garnish (optional)

Preparation

Heat a pan over medium heat and melt the coconut oil. Add the minced garlic and cook for one minute until fragrant. Remove garlic to small bowl.

Add the scallops and cook for about one minute on each side until they are firm and opaque.

Remove scallops from pan and set aside. Add the lemon juice and previously cooked garlic to the hot coconut oil in the pan. Season to taste with salt and pepper.

Serve the scallops on a bed of steamed or roasted vegetables with the lemon and garlic sauce on top. Spinach and asparagus go very well with scallops. Additionally, sprinkle some fresh parsley or chives on top if desired.

Baba-ghanoush

<u>Serves 8</u>

Ingredients

2 large eggplants
2 garlic cloves, minced
2 Tbsp fresh lemon juice
1 Tbsp extra virgin olive oil
1 tsp cumin
Salt and pepper to taste
Fresh parsley, optional, for garnishing

Preparation

Preheat oven to 400 F. Prick the skin of the eggplants several times with a fork and roast for about 35 minutes in the oven on a cookie sheet. Put the roasted eggplants in a bowl of cold water, wait a bit and then peel off the skin.

Place the roasted eggplant, garlic, lemon juice, tahini, olive oil, and cumin in a blender and blend until smooth. Season to taste with salt and pepper. Cool in the refrigerator and serve with extra olive oil on top and fresh parsley.

Zucchini and Carrot Frittata

Serves 4

Ingredients

2 Tbsp coconut oil
8 eggs
1 cup carrots, peeled & sliced
2 sliced zucchinis
1 sliced red bell pepper
2 Tbsp fresh parsley
Salt and pepper to taste

Preparation

Heat an ovenable pan over medium-low heat. Add the oil and carrot slices and cook, turning once, until soft, about 8 minutes.

Add the zucchini and red bell pepper slices and cook for another 4 minutes.

While it cooks, whisk the eggs in a bowl, making sure to incorporate a lot of air in the mixture (this makes the frittata light and airy). Turn oven to the broil setting.

Season the egg mixture with salt and pepper and add to the cooking veggies.

Cook on low heat until just set, about 10 minutes. Finish the frittata until golden under a heated broiler. Check every 2-3 minutes until done.

Cut the finished frittata into wedges and serve with fresh parsley.

Braised Oxtail

Serves 4

Ingredients

2 oxtails, each one cut in 4 sections

1/2 cup chopped carrots

1/2 cup diced onions

1/2 cup chopped celery

1/2 cup chopped leeks

4 Tbsp tallow or lard (may use coconut oil)

1 lb tomatoes, whole

8 sprigs fresh thyme

2 bay leaves

4 crushed garlic cloves

1 cup red wine (optional)

4 1/2 cups chicken or beef stock (see recipe on page 195)

Vegetable garnish

1 finely diced carrot

1 finely diced onion

2 finely diced celery stalks

1/2 leek, finely diced

4 small tomatoes, finely diced

2 Tbsp chopped parsley

Preparation

Preheat oven to 350 F. Heat the lard or tallow in a pan and brown the oxtail pieces on each side. Remove the oxtail and brown the vegetables for the main braising liquid (carrots, celery, onions and leeks). Make sure you stir and scrape off any meat residue in the bottom of the pan (this improves the broth).

Add the whole tomatoes, thyme, bay leaves and garlic and cook for a couple of minutes.

Put the oxtail and browned vegetables in a Dutch oven and add the wine (if desired).

Boil the wine at high heat until almost evaporated, and then add stock to cover the oxtail entirely. If not using wine, just add the stock directly.

Bring the whole preparation to a simmer, cover and place in oven to braise for about 1 1/2 to 2 hours.

After cooking, many chefs will strain the liquid to remove the small pieces of cooked and mushy vegetables for appearance reasons. It's up to you whether you remove them. Do remove the bay leaves, however.

Blanch the garnishing vegetables (except tomatoes) in boiling water for about 4 minutes. Place the blanched vegetables in the oxtail preparation and simmer for about 2 minutes. Enjoy this sophisticated but simple dish!

Waldorf Salad

<u>Serves 4</u>

Ingredients

1 cup chopped walnuts

1 cup diced celery

1 cup fresh grapes and/or leftover chicken, optional

2 red apples, cored and sliced

1/4 cup green onions

2 Tbsp lemon juice

8 Tbsp Paleo mayonnaise (recipe on page 168) or coconut milk

Romaine lettuce leaves for serving

Salt and pepper to taste

Preparation

Mix the mayonnaise and lemon juice in a large bowl and season to taste. Add the walnuts, celery, apples, green onions as well as grapes and chicken (if using) and mix it all together. Serve the salad on a bed of romaine lettuce.

Cooking Whole Fish and Grilled Trout

Because of their fat content, salmon and trout are the best fishes to cook whole, because the fat makes them more forgiving if overcooked a little. Sea bass and grouper will also work nicely.

Put the fish in a snug-fitting dish so the cooking juices can remain in contact with the fish while cooking. Complex flavors can be developed by putting vegetables under the fish and inside the cavity while cooking. Try lemon slices, fennel, garlic, onion, parsley, dill, carrots, thyme, and rosemary. Be creative!

It's also very Paleo to eat the fish whole - eat everything, including the eyes; and, keep the bones to make fumet (fish stock).

Lemon Dill Trout

Serves 2

Ingredients

Two whole trout (or other fish if desired), scaled, gutted and cleaned
2 Tbsp coconut oil
1 bunch fresh flat leaf parsley
1 bunch fresh dill
Zest of one lemon
2 lemons, one sliced and the other halved
Salt and pepper to taste

Preparation

Preheat your broiler.

Slash the sides of your fishes about 8 times each side with a knife so the oil can seep in.

Rub the trout with coconut oil and season with salt and pepper.

Stuff the cavity with chopped parsley, dill and lemon slices.

Put the fish on a baking rack on a pan to catch drippings.

Add generous amount of coconut oil to the fish to form a wonderful golden crust and sprinkle the lemon zest on top of the fish and.

You can place the lemon halves on the baking tray too.

Grill about 6 inches away from the heat source, for about 6 minutes on each side.

Squeeze the roasted lemons on the fish before serving.

Duck Confit (preserved duck)

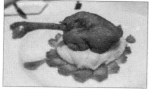

Serves 4

Ingredients

4 duck legs with thighs

4 duck wings

4 cups duck fat

3 Tbsp salt

4 garlic cloves, very finely minced

1 onion, sliced

6 sprigs thyme

3 sprigs rosemary

Pepper to taste

Preparation

Mix the salt, garlic, onion, thyme, rosemary and pepper together.

Using a dish large enough to hold all the duck pieces in a single layer sprinkle 1/3 of the spice mixture on the bottom.

Put the duck pieces in the dish, skin side up on the spice mixture bed.

Sprinkle the remaining 2/3 of the spice mixture evenly on the duck.

Cover and refrigerate for about 24 to 48 hours. When ready, preheat oven to 225 F and rinse salt from the duck and arrange the duck in a baking dish in a tight single layer.

Melt the duck fat and pour over the duck. Make sure it covers the meat entirely.

Put in the oven for 2 to 4 hours until the meat can easily be pulled from the bone.

The duck confit is now ready and can be stored in the fat where it will stay good for weeks.

Carrot Confit

<u>Serves 4</u>

Ingredients

2 lbs carrots

Zest of 2 lemons

Juice 2 lemons

4 cloves garlic, very finely minced

3 sprigs thyme

1 cup melted duck fat (you can use any animal fat or coconut oil)

Preparation

Preheat oven to 275 F.

Prepare your carrots by cutting them in 1-inch pieces or leave them whole if they will all fit flat in your baking dish.

Mix the zest, lemon juice, garlic, thyme and fat together and pour over carrots. You want to cover the carrots completely. Add fat if necessary.
Put in the oven for about 2 hours.

Remove from oven. At this point, the carrots will be soft and delicious.

As an optional step before serving, brown the carrots in a large skillet with the fat mixture that was used to cook them. This will create a crispy exterior and a tender interior.

Traditional Chicken Liver Pâté

<u>Serves 2</u>

Ingredients

1/2 lb chicken livers

1 clove garlic, minced

3 thin slices bacon (no preservatives and naturally seasoned), chopped in cubes

1 large diced onion

3/4 cup coconut oil

4 Tbsp chopped parsley

3 Tbsp sherry or favorite vinegar

Fresh nutmeg (optional)

Salt and pepper to taste

Preparation

Heat a large pan to medium high heat and cook the bacon for about 3 minutes. Add the onion, garlic and 1/4 cup of the coconut oil and soften for about 3 or 4 minutes.

Prepare the livers by cutting out the white stringy part.

Add the livers to the pot and cook for about 7 to 10 minutes with a little more of the cooking fat. Once cooked through, add sherry, parsley and salt, pepper and fresh nutmeg to taste.

Remove from heat and pour mixture in a blender or food processor and blend until smooth.
Pour the mixture in a serving dish.

Pour the remaining cooking fat (melted) over the pâté evenly.

Cover and put in the refrigerator to cool until the fat hardens.

Basil, Cinnamon, Cranberry Chicken and Heart Pâté

<u>Serves 10</u>

This makes a huge batch. So if you don't plan on eating it all, make half the recipe.

Ingredients

1 cup duck fat (use any animal fat, duck is really good in this case)
2 1/2 lb chicken or pork liver (or a mix of both)
1 pork heart
2 large onions, diced
1 garlic clove, minced
1 cup chopped fresh basil
5 tsp freshly ground cinnamon
4 Tbsp raw unpasteurized apple cider vinegar
1 1/2 cup fresh or frozen cranberries, divided
Salt and pepper to taste.

Preparation

Heat a medium-to-large pot and soften the onions for 3 or 4 minutes with half the duck fat. Add the garlic when onions are almost soft and cook until the garlic become fragrant, about 1 minute. Prepare the livers and heart by removing the stringy white part and cutting down to similar sizes.

Add the livers and heart part to the pot with the onions and cook on medium heat for 7 to 10 minutes. You can add a bit more duck fat at this point and season with salt and pepper.

Add the sherry or vinegar, basil and half the cranberries.

Pour the mixture in a blender or food processor and blend until smooth with the cinnamon. Unless you have a very large food processor, you'll have to do it in multiple batches.

Cut remaining cranberries in half.

Combine the pâté and halved cranberries in a large dish.

Taste and adjust seasonings to taste (cinnamon, salt and pepper).

Melt the remaining duck fat in a small pot and pour on top of the finished pâté.

Cover the dish and put in the refrigerator to cool and harden for about 1 or 2 hours.

Ginger Citrus Roast Chicken

Serves 4

Ingredients

5 Tbsp coconut oil (or lard or tallow)

3 lemons or 4 limes

2 oranges

1 whole chicken, about 4 1/2 lbs

3 Tbsp grated fresh ginger

Salt and pepper to taste

Preparation

Preheat your oven to 425 F. Grate the zest 1 orange and orange lemon and then cut them in quarter.

Wipe the chicken dry and place it in a roasting pan.

Mix 1 Tbsp of the grated ginger with the citrus zest. Rub the citrus mixture in the chicken cavity with some added salt and pepper if wanted. Add the quartered lemon and orange inside the cavity. Juice the remaining lemons and orange with the remaining 2 Tbsp ginger and also add the melted coconut oil. Brush the chicken with the mixture. Put in the oven for 15 minutes; after 15 minutes, baste the chicken and reduce the heat to 375 F. After another 25 minutes, baste again, turn the chicken on its breast and cook for another 25 minutes.

At this point, check doneness of the chicken by verifying the juices run clear when you cut the thickest part of the breast. You can also use a meat thermometer (should be 160 F in the breast and at least 170 F in the thigh).

When ready, remove from oven and let the chicken rest for 15 minutes. Garnish with extra citrus wedges if desired on a bed of steamed vegetables or spinach. Use the citrus, coconut oil and ginger cooking juice as a sauce.

Paleo Spaghetti

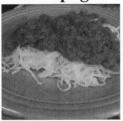

<u>Serves 2</u>

Use one medium to large spaghetti squash for 2 people.

Ingredients

1/2 lb ground grass-fed beef
1 Tbsp coconut oil
1/2 large onion, chopped and diced
1 1/2 cloves garlic, minced
1 1/2 carrots, diced
1 celery stick, diced
1 tsp dried oregano
1 Tbsp tomato paste
1 small bay leaf
The equivalent of 1 can whole meaty tomatoes
Optional: 2-4 Tbsp full-fat coconut milk (makes the sauce less acidic)
Salt and pepper to taste
Fresh parsley for garnishing

Preparation

Heat a large Dutch oven or pot and add cooking fat. You can use less fat if your ground beef has a high fat content, it's really a question of taste. Cook the ground beef for about 5 minutes. Remove the meat with a slotted spoon and set aside.

Use the same Dutch oven or pot to cook the other ingredients (carrots, celery, onion, garlic and oregano). Cook the vegetables until soft over medium heat. Add the tomatoes, tomato paste, ground beef and bay leaf. Season with salt and pepper if desired. You can also add some chili or hot pepper flakes for more heat. Bring to a boil and then reduce to a simmer for about 45 minutes.

In the meantime, heat your oven to 350 F. Cut your spaghetti squash in half length-wise, remove and discard the seeds. Put the halves cut side down on a baking sheet and put in the oven for about 28 to 35 minutes. Check on them around the 25-minute mark with a fork. It should easily break up to form pasta-like strands. Make sure not to overcook them because they will become mushy and won't make "pasta".

Once your Bolognese sauce is cooked, you can add about 1/4 cup to a cup of coconut milk. This will make the sauce less acidic.

You can now pour a generous amount of the sauce directly on the squash halves so that it forms its own bowl or you can break the squashes in strands yourself and serve on a plate with the sauce. Garnish with fresh parsley and enjoy!

Hungarian Beef Goulash

This recipe serves about 2-3 people. I suggest that you make more and that you freeze the leftovers. Prepared stews are always good to have around for the times that cooking is not an option.

Ingredients

Cooking oil (lard or tallow are good choices)
1/2 lb stewing beef, cut in cubes (grass-fed beef, ideally)
2 medium onions, sliced
1 large garlic clove, crushed and minced
1 bell pepper, sliced
2 Tbsp paprika (this can be adjusted to taste, don't be scared to use a lot of it)
2 tsp caraway seeds
1 can chopped tomatoes (fresh tomatoes are even better)
1 1/2 cups of bone stock (beef stock is best, but anything will do. See recipe on page 195)
Chopped parsley for garnishing

Preparation

Preheat your oven to 350 F. You can also use a crock-pot, on low temperature.

Brown the beef cubes in a pot with the cooking oil. Put the beef aside and now brown and soften the onions. Add the garlic and bell pepper and cook to soften: about 5 minutes over medium heat.

Put the beef back in the pot and add the spices, tomatoes and stock.

Put a lid on the pot and transfer to the hot oven or put the preparation in your crock-pot.

Let it cook for about 2 to 2 1/2 hours, until the beef is fork-tender.

"Butter" Chicken

<u>Serves 4</u>

Ingredients

4 Tbsp coconut oil, divided

2 1/8 lbs chicken, cut in chunks

2 tsp garam masala

2 tsp paprika

2 tsp ground coriander

1 Tbsp grated fresh ginger

1/4 tsp chili powder (adjust to taste)

1 cinnamon stick

6 bruised cardamom pods

1 can of tomato puree (you can easily puree your own tomatoes if they are meaty enough)

3/4 cup coconut milk

1 Tbsp fresh lemon juice

Preparation

Heat a pan, add the first 2 Tbsp of coconut oil and stir-fry the chicken chunks. You can cook them in

2 batches if your pan is too small. Remove the chicken from the pan.

Add the second 2 Tbsp of coconut oil and stir in the spices. Slowly return the heat to the pan (for a minute or two) until you can smell the aroma.

Put the chicken back in the pan and stir so you mix in all the spices with the chicken.

At this point, add the tomatoes and simmer for about 15 minutes. Stir from time to time.

Add the coconut milk and lemon juice and let it simmer for another 5 minutes.

Enjoy without guilt! Garnish with fresh herbs and a stick of cinnamon for extra fanciness points.

Butternut Squash Soup

<u>Serves 2</u>

Ingredients

1 medium butternut squash
1 can of coconut milk
Sea salt and freshly ground black pepper to taste
Any fresh or dried herb you have on hand

Preparation

Preheat your oven to 350 F.

Cut your squash length-wise and remove the seeds.
Place the halves, cut side down, on a baking sheet
and place in the oven for about 45 minutes. IF the
flesh is fork tender, it's ready. If it's not quite
tender yet, continue to bake and check in 10-
minute increments.

Remove squash from oven and cool on a rack. Scoop out the cooked flesh in a saucepan and add about 3/4 of a can of coconut milk per squash. Place squash in a food processor or blender and puree until smooth or mash with a potato masher in a large bowl.

Adjust the consistency of the squash by adding coconut milk if needed. Season with salt and pepper to taste. Place soup in serving bowls. To garnish, sprinkle or grate a bit of fresh nutmeg over top of soup. You can also add some grated fresh ginger or garlic for a nice spin on the taste.

For more impressive presentation, drizzle additional coconut milk in a spiral on the served bowls to create a white swirl.

Almond-Crusted Salmon

<u>Serves 4</u>

Ingredients

2 Tbsp Coconut oil

1/2 cup almond meal

1/4 tsp coriander

1/8 tsp cumin

4 salmon fillets

2 tsp lemon juice

Sea salt

Fresh ground black pepper

Preparation

Preheat the oven to 500F.

Combine almond meal, coriander and cumin in a small bowl.

Melt Coconut oil in a nonstick pan.

Spritz the salmon with the lemon juice and season with salt and pepper.

Coat each fillet with the almond meal mixture. Place salmon, skin side down, in the oiled pan.

Bake at 500 F for 12 minutes or until flesh flakes easily with a fork.

Barbecue Juneau Shrimp

<u>Serves 6</u>
Ingredients
1/4 cup virgin olive oil
3 garlic gloves minced
2 Tbsp lemon juice
1/8 tsp of paprika
Dash of cayenne pepper to taste
2 1/2 lbs shelled shrimp with tail left on
Lime wedges and parsley

Preparation

Mix olive oil, spices and lemon juice in a bowl.
Fire up grill. Brush shrimp with mixture, place on
hot grill, turn once (1-2 minutes per side) and
remove. Place lime wedges and parsley on top
after completed.

Bison Chili

<u>Serves 6</u>

Chef's note: you don't have to use bison; lean ground beef will work but bison has more flavor and a better nutrition profile than regular beef. Venison and Elk are also great in this recipe and very lean.

Ingredients
1 Tbsp coconut oil
1 3/4 lbs ground bison
1/2 onion, chopped
2 1/2 cups chopped celery
2 cloves garlic
12 oz jar of salsa
1 8 oz can of diced tomatoes
2 tsp cumin
2 tsp chili powder
2 tsp thyme leaves, fresh
2 tsp sea salt
1/4 cup mild green chilies

Preparation

Sauté over medium heat the onions, celery and garlic until onions are translucent—about 3 or 4 minutes.

Then add the meat, cumin, thyme, and chili powder.

Stir while this cooks for about 5 to 6 minutes.
Then pour in the salsa, tomatoes and salt.
Add about a 1/4-cup of mild green chilies.
Let this simmer for at least an hour before serving.

Simple Stuffed Portobellos

<u>Serves 2</u>

Ingredients

2 Portobello mushroom caps

1 can yellow fin tuna in oil, drained. (If using fresh tuna, sear or cook to desired temperature)

1/2 medium avocado

Pinch of cayenne pepper or chili flakes (or hot sauce), to taste

Sea salt, optional

Fresh or dried garlic, optional

Mixed-color peppercorns, optional

Preparation

Lightly grill, sauté, or roast the Portobello caps, if desired, and set aside.

Mash and mix all other ingredients together in a bowl, then and stuff into Portobello caps.

For a sweeter touch, sprinkle in some raisins or currants. For an Indian flavor, add in curry and walnuts.

Can be served at room temperature, but serve immediately to avoid the darkening of the avocado.

Cilantro Turkey Burgers

Serves 4

Ingredients

1 lb ground turkey (lean)
1 cup chopped cilantro
1/4 cup chopped red onion
2 tsp minced garlic
3/4 tsp salt
1/4 tsp pepper
Olive oil for basting

Preparation

Combine all ingredients in a bowl and mix well.

Divide into 4 portions and shape into patties.

Grill/broil until cooked to desired doneness.

Paleo Pizza

Serves 4

Chef's notes: This is a basic pizza recipe. You can alter it and add whatever veggies and meats you like to make your favorite style of pizza.

Ingredients
2 tsp olive oil, divided
1 cup almond flour
3 Tbsp cashew butter
1/3 cup egg whites
1/2 cup chopped onion
2 cloves minced garlic
1 chopped red pepper
1/2 cup halved grape tomatoes
1 large Italian sausage, cut in 1/2" slices (double check to ensure low sodium and that there are no artificial preservatives or additives)
1/2 cup marinara sauce or crushed tomatoes
1/2 tsp oregano
1/2 tsp fennel seed

Preparation

Mix almond flour, cashew butter, and egg whites in a small bowl. This makes the dough.

Cover a pizza-baking sheet with 2 tsp of olive oil, and then spread the "dough" mixture over it, making a 1/4-inch thick crust. Preheat the oven to 250 F.

In a skillet brown the sliced sausage. Once browned, remove from skillet and place in small bowl. Add the garlic, onions, and red pepper to the skillet. Sauté the veggies 3-5 minutes over medium heat until onions are just translucent. You do not want them to be too soft.

Cover the dough with the marinara sauce, and then add the meat and all the vegetables except the tomatoes. Add the oregano and fennel seed. Place in oven and bake for 30 minutes at 300 F.

Remove pizza from oven and add the halved tomatoes. Serve using a spatula to remove the slices from the pan.

Hot Cilantro Shrimp

Serves 2

Chef's notes: Which skewer to use is always a debate; wooden skewers burn if not soaked in water for at least 20 minutes before using, and metal skewers can burn YOU if not handled carefully after grilling. Be careful.

Instructions

1 lb large or jumbo shrimp, peeled and deveined
½ cup cilantro, rinsed and coarsely chopped (about 1 cup)
4 jalapeño peppers, seeded and coarsely chopped (for hotter shrimp, leave the seeds in)
4 scallions, chopped
3 cloves garlic, chopped
Metal or bamboo skewers (2 for each kebab)
1 tsp ground black pepper
1 tsp ground cumin
1/2 cup extra virgin olive oil
1/4 cup fresh lime juice

Preparation

Thread the shrimp onto 2 parallel skewers, using 2 skewers for each kebab. Arrange the kebabs in a nonreactive baking dish.

Set aside 3 Tbsp of the cilantro for the garlic cilantro sauce. Place the remaining cilantro, the jalapenos, scallions, chopped garlic, salt, black pepper, and cumin in a food processor and finely chop. With the machine running, add 1/4 cup olive oil and lime juice through the feed tube and purée to bright green paste. Pour this marinade over the shrimp and let them marinate in the refrigerator, covered, for 30 minutes.

Heat remaining oil in a saucepan over medium heat, add reserved cilantro and cook until the garlic is fragrant, about 2 minutes. Keep the cilantro sauce warm until ready to use.

Set up the grill for direct grilling and preheat to high.

When ready to cook, drain the marinade from the kebabs and discard the marinade. Place the shrimp kebabs on the hot grate and grill until just cooked through, 1 to 3 minutes per side, basting with the garlic cilantro sauce. When shrimp are done they will turn pinkish white and feel firm to the touch.

Transfer to plates, pour any of the remaining sauce over them, and serve with lime wedges.

Paleo Meatloaf

<u>Serves 3-4</u>

Ingredients

1 1/2 lbs lean ground beef

1 cup almond milk

1/4 tsp dried sage

1/2 tsp salt

1/2 tsp dry mustard

1/4 tsp fresh ground pepper

2 cloves garlic, minced

1 small onion, finely chopped

1/2 cup chopped cabbage

1/2 cup Paleo barbecue sauce (optional)

Preparation

Preheat oven to 350 degrees.

Combine all ingredients except BBQ Sauce in a large bowl, and mix.

Place mixture into an ungreased loaf pan or shape into a loaf on an un-greased baking pan.

Pour sauce over the top of the meatloaf.

Bake uncovered for 1 to 1 1/4 hours until an internal temperature of 160 degrees is achieved (or until no pink in the center).

Let stand for 5 minutes, then slice and serve.

Salmon with Coconut Cream Sauce

Serves 1-2

Ingredients

1 lb salmon filet (wild caught)
3/4 medium shallot, diced
3 cloves garlic, minced
2 tsp olive oil
2 Tbsp fresh basil, chopped
Zest from one lemon
Lemon juice, from one lemon
1/2 cup coconut milk
Salt and Pepper to taste

Preparation

Preheat oven to 350 degrees.

Place salmon on a foil-lined baking sheet and sprinkle with salt and pepper.

In a non-stick skillet, sauté garlic and shallot in olive oil.

Add lemon zest and lemon juice.

Add coconut milk slowly and bring liquid to a low boil.

Reduce heat and add basil.

Pour over salmon and bake for 10-15 minutes or until fish flakes easily.

Serve warm.

Vegetable Kabobs

Serves 2

Ingredients

4 mushrooms

1 zucchini, sliced thick

1/2 a head of 1 cauliflower, pulled apart

1 red bell pepper, cut into large pieces

2 carrots, sliced thick

1 onion, quartered

2-inch piece of fresh ginger, peeled

2 cloves garlic

1/2 cups Paleo vinaigrette (recipe on page 156)

2 cups water

1/2 Tbsp cayenne

1 Tbsp basil

1 Tbsp oregano

Wooden skewers

Preparation

Wash and prepare first six vegetables.
Blend remaining ingredients and pour over
vegetables in bowl.

Marinate overnight in refrigerator.

Soak wooden skewers in water for 15 minutes to
avoid burning.

Prepare grill.

Put vegetables onto skewers and place on grill for
about 10 minutes. Turn frequently.

Serve warm.

Salad Dressings and Vinaigrettes

<u>Chef's notes on general preparation guidelines:</u>

For a classic oil-based vinaigrette, you will want to put the vinegar used in a bowl with the spices and seasonings. Adding salt before the oil is important because it will get a chance to dissolve in the vinegar. You'll then want to slowly drizzle the oil into the bowl while whisking vigorously at the same time. The whole process can of course be done with the help of a blender or a food processor.

Dijon mustard is often included in vinaigrette recipes, it helps with the emulsion of the oil with the vinegar and gives a nice taste, but it can always be omitted. You can also make your own mustard to be sure you don't eat any unwanted ingredient or preservative.

Always wait until the last minute to dress the salad so the vegetables don't become soggy.

Lemon Vinaigrette

Excellent with all kinds of salad, and especially good with smoked salmon salad.

<u>Serves 4</u>

Ingredients

3 Tbsp fresh lime or lemon juice
1/2 tsp Dijon mustard (optional)
6 Tbsp extra-virgin olive oil
Sea salt and freshly ground black pepper to taste

Preparation

Follow the general preparation technique by combining all the ingredients except the oil and then adding the oil slowly while whisking vigorously. Using a blender will help to emulsify the vinaigrette. Shake well before using.

Balsamic Vinaigrette

This is a classic of Italian cuisine and also acts as a proper marinade for your meat. It's also fabulous when drizzled on cooked vegetables.

<u>Serves 12</u>
Ingredients
3/4 cup balsamic vinegar
1 crushed clove of garlic
1 tsp dried oregano
2 tsp Dijon mustard, optional
3/4 cup extra-virgin olive oil
Sea salt and freshly ground black pepper to taste

Preparation
Put all the ingredients in a jar that has a lid. Close the lid tight and shake well to combine all the ingredients.

Crushed Tomato Vinaigrette

This dressing is good for all kinds of salads and really great on grilled fish or chicken.

<u>Serves 8</u>

Ingredients

1 quantity of the classic lemon vinaigrette

4 oz cherry tomatoes

1 crushed clove of garlic

Preparation

Add all ingredients in a blender and process to a smooth purée. You can thin it with a little water if necessary.

Sauce Vierge Warm Dressing

Sauce vierge means virgin sauce and this warm dressing is sure to please taste buds that are still virgin to this sauce. It's excellent when served on warm vegetables or fish.

<u>Serves 8</u>

Ingredients

1 crushed garlic clove

1 finely chopped shallot or small onion

7 Tbsp olive oil

1/2 cup peeled and finely diced tomatoes

Juice of 1 lemon

2 tsp chopped basil

Preparation

Place the garlic and chopped shallot or onion in a pot with the oil or clarified butter and heat the ingredients over low heat until soft, but without frying. Add the tomatoes and cook for about 5 minutes and then add the lemon juice and chopped basil and stir. Season to taste and serve hot.

Caesar Dressing

<u>Serves 8</u>

Ingredients

1 Tbsp lemon juice

2 Tbsp Paleo mayonnaise (recipe on page 168)

1/2 cup extra-virgin olive oil

6 garlic cloves, minced

1 Tbsp Dijon mustard

Minced anchovy fillets

Sea salt and freshly ground black pepper to taste

Preparation

Using a blender, process the lemon juice, garlic and mustard. Add the Paleo mayonnaise and blend again. Slowly add the olive oil while the blender is in motion. Use a spatula to scrape all that delicious dressing in a bowl, season with salt and pepper, add more lemon juice to taste and minced anchovy fillets to taste.

Raspberry-Walnut Vinaigrette

Serves 5

Ingredients

3 Tbsp raspberry vinegar

1/2 tsp Dijon mustard, optional

6 Tbsp walnut oil

2 Tbsp chopped walnuts

Sea salt and freshly ground black pepper to taste

Preparation

Make the dressing as you would for classic lemon juice vinaigrette (recipe on page 158) and add the chopped walnuts at the end.

Orange & Rosemary Vinaigrette

Serves 4

Ingredients

3 Tbsp fresh lime or lemon juice

1/2 tsp Dijon mustard, optional

6 Tbsp extra-virgin olive oil

Grated zest and juice of 1 orange

1 tsp chopped rosemary, fresh

Sea salt and freshly ground black pepper to taste

Preparation

Prepare classic lemon juice vinaigrette (recipe on page 158) and add the grated zest and juice of one orange and 1 tsp chopped rosemary. Let infuse overnight for a better taste.

Ginger Asian Vinaigrette

This vinaigrette is especially good on bitter greens or salads featuring roasted beets.

<u>Serves 4</u>

Ingredients

3 Tbsp rice vinegar

1 large piece fresh ginger

5 Tbsp extra-virgin olive oil

1 Tbsp sesame oil

Sea salt and freshly ground black pepper to taste

Preparation

Peel the piece of ginger and grate with a box grater, then squeeze the resulting grated ginger to obtain about 1 Tbsp ginger juice and discard the grated ginger. Whisk together in a bowl the grated ginger juice and the rice vinegar. Whisk while incorporating the olive oil. Add the sesame oil and season to taste.

Roasted Chili Dressing

This is a dressing with a bold taste so it will go well with bold salads featuring strong herbs or root vegetables.

Serves 5

Ingredients

3 red chilies

6 Tbsp extra-virgin olive oil

3 1/2 Tbsp lemon juice

1 bunch of finely chopped mint leaves – about 1 fistful

Sea salt and freshly ground black pepper to taste

Preparation

Prick the chilies with the tip of a knife so they don't explode while roasting. Place them under the broiler until well roasted and skin is completely charred. You can also use tongs and hold them close to the flame of a gas stove.

Once roasted, put plastic wrap on top for a couple of minutes so they steam and the charred skin is easy to peel off. Peel the chilies, open them, remove the seeds and finely chop the flesh. Mix thoroughly in a bowl with the oil, lemon juice, and mint and season to taste.

Paleo Mayonnaise

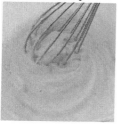

<u>Yields 1 1/4 cups</u>

Ingredients

2 egg yolks

1 tsp mustard, this is optional

3 tsp lemon juice

1/2 cup olive oil

1/2 cup coconut oil

Preparation

Put the yolks in a bowl (or blender/food processor) with the mustard (optional) and 1 tsp lemon juice. Mix those ingredients together.

While whisking vigorously (blender or food processor on low) add the oil very slowly, even drop by drop in the beginning. You're creating an emulsion and if you add too much oil at once, it will separate and will be very hard to save. Whisk non-stop, using a towel under the bowl to help stabilize the bowl.

As you add more oil, the emulsion will form, the mayonnaise will start to thicken, and you can pour the oil faster at this point.

When all the oil is incorporated and the mayonnaise is thick, add the rest of the lemon juice and season to taste with salt and pepper.
Enjoy without guilt. Refrigerate leftover mayonnaise!

Notes:
You can extend this recipe with spices, fresh herbs (dill is delicious in it), garlic or even chopped pickles for a tartar sauce.

As for the technique, you may use a blender, a food processor or a whisk. The technique is basically the same for all those methods, so I explained it in a way applicable for the three methods.

The coconut mayonnaise is made with half olive oil because it would become way too hard in the refrigerator. I don't recommend a full olive oil mayonnaise unless you use a light tasting olive oil because the flavor will be too pronounced.

Guacamole

Chef's Notes: Avocados darken quickly when exposed to air. This does not affect the taste but it is unattractive. You can slow the darkening by storing in lemon or lime juice or as directed below by keeping the avocado in direct contact with plastic wrap.

Yields 2 1/2 cups

Ingredients

3 medium avocados or 4 small ones

1 firm tomato, finely diced

1/2 a white onion

1/2 cup chopped cilantro

2 Tbsp fresh lemon or lime juice

Optional salt and pepper to taste

Preparation

Open the avocados and scoop out the flesh. An easy way is to cut it length-wise around the pit and then using a chef's knife strike the pit and twist the knife so you can easily remove the pit and scoop out the flesh.

Mash the flesh with a fork, leaving it as chunky or smooth as you prefer.

Stir in the other ingredients.

Enjoy right away or store in the refrigerator. If storing in the refrigerator, place guacamole in a bowl covered with plastic wrap. Plastic should touch entire surface of the guacamole so it minimizes air contact and browning of the surface of the guacamole.

Mexican Salsa Verde

<u>Serves 4</u>

Chef's Notes: The tomatillos are usually roasted, but you could also simmer them for about 5 minutes for "close enough" results.

Ingredients

1/2 cup onion, chopped

1 1/2 lb green tomatillos, husks removed

1/2 cup cilantro, chopped

2 Tbsp lime juice

2 jalapeño peppers, seeded and chopped

Salt and pepper to taste

Preparation

Cut the tomatillos length-wise and roast them either on the grill or for about 6 minutes under the broiler until the skin is a little dark.

Put the roasted tomatillos, onion, cilantro, lime juice and jalapeño in a blender or food processor. Blend or process until you obtain a smooth purée. Place in the refrigerator to cool and enjoy.

Condiment Recipes

Simple Ketchup

<u>Yields 1 1/2 cups</u>

Ingredients

1 can (6 ounces) tomato paste

2 Tbsp vinegar or lemon juice

1/4 tsp dry mustard

1/3 cup water

1/4 tsp cinnamon

1/4 tsp salt

1 pinch ground cloves

1 pinch ground allspice

1/8 tsp cayenne pepper, optional

Preparation

Simply combine all the ingredients in a bowl and whisk well to combine. Refrigerate overnight to let the flavors develop.

Rich and Deep-Flavored Ketchup (Traditional)

Yields about 2 cups

Ingredients

1 lb fresh plum tomatoes + 1 lb canned plum tomatoes or 2 lbs fresh plum tomatoes, chopped

1 large onion, chopped

1/2 fennel bulb, chopped

1 celery stick, cut in cubes

Chopped fresh 1 in. piece of ginger

2 cloves garlic, roughly chopped

1/2 red chili, seeded and chopped finely

Large bunch of fresh basil, picked leaves and chopped stalks (separated)

1 Tbsp coriander seeds

2 cloves garlic

1 tsp freshly ground black pepper

Extra virgin olive oil

3/4 cup + 2 Tbsp red wine, balsamic or apple cider vinegar

Sea salt to taste

Preparation

Place the onion, fennel and celery in a large saucepan with some olive oil, the ginger, garlic, chopped chili, basil stalks, coriander seeds and garlic cloves and season with salt and the black pepper.

Over low heat, cook for about 12 minutes, until the vegetables have softened, stirring occasionally. Add 1 1/2 cups of water and the tomatoes. Let simmer gently until the liquid is reduced by one half. Add the basil leaves, pour the sauce in a blender or food processor and process until very smooth. Strain the sauce through a sieve into a new or cleaned saucepan and add the vinegar.

Simmer again until it reaches the desired ketchup consistency. Adjust the seasoning to taste. Cool in the refrigerator and enjoy. This ketchup recipe can be bottled in sterilized jars and kept for up to 6 months in a cool dark place.

Simple Mustard

This is a very basic mustard recipe that can be prepared on demand when you feel like having some mustard. It only takes one part water to one part mustard powder and you'll get nice and hot mustard. Let it stand for a bit and the heat will reduce. You can play around with the seasoning and use different herbs and spices to create different versions. Vinegars or lemon juice will also add a pleasant tanginess. Store in a glass jar.

Yields about ½ cup

Ingredients

1/2 cup mustard powder

1/4 cup water

1/4 cup white wine vinegar

Sea salt to taste

Preparation

Combine the mustard powder, water and vinegar in a bowl and mix well.

If desired, add a bit of chopped fresh parsley or basil, lemon or lime zest and a tablespoon or two of your favorite vinegar.

Let the mustard stand for about 15 minutes before enjoying.

The mustard will be thinner and much stronger than what you purchase in the grocery store.

Consider using a small quantity brushed on bread for sandwiches or as an additive to other condiments in this book, for example barbecue sauce (recipe on page 194)

Whole-grain mustard

Feel free to play around with this recipe by adding any of your favorite fresh herbs. Sundried tomatoes and fresh basil are excellent additions.

Yields about 1 ¼ cups

Ingredients

1/4 cup yellow mustard seeds

1/4 cup brown mustard seeds

1 cup white wine or water

4 tsp mustard powder

1/4 cup white wine vinegar

1/2 tsp sea salt

Preparation

Soak the mustard seeds in the white wine or water overnight.

Place the seeds and soaking liquid in a blender or food processor with the mustard powder, vinegar and sea salt. Process to a paste-like consistency. Put in a glass jar, cover and refrigerate for about 4 days before serving.

Lacto-Fermented Cucumber Relish

This traditional recipe uses lacto-fermentation to create the acidic taste and probiotic value of that food.

Additional flavors to possibly add are dill, garlic and mustard seeds. The following recipe uses fresh dill. You can use a vegetable starter culture like those available www.culturesforhealth.com to ensure success of the lacto-fermentation, but I find that simply using sea salt yields great results.

<u>Yields about 8 cups</u>

Ingredients

   4 large cucumbers, chopped finely

   2 Tbsp fresh dill or 2 tsp dried

   2 Tbsp sea salt

Preparation

In a bowl, mix the chopped cucumbers, dill and sea salt.

In a quart-sized glass jar equipped with a lid, pack the cucumber mixture tightly with a wooden spoon or your fist, making sure to extract the most water out of the mixture. You want the water to cover the mixture for the fermentation process to happen and to prevent mold from forming.

Add some filtered water if needed. Make sure that there is at least 1 inch of room between the liquid and the top of the jar, as the mixture will expand during the fermentation time.

Cover the glass jar tightly with the lid and leave in a warm place for 2 to 5 days. You can taste the relish during the fermentation process to know if it's ready or not.

When ready, transfer to the refrigerator and enjoy.

Horseradish

Horseradish is the name of a root vegetable of the Brassica family used to prepare a horseradish condiment often simply called horseradish or prepared horseradish. It has a quite pungent and hot taste and goes well with roasted red meat or mixed in some mayonnaise.

Today most prepared horseradish is made with vinegar, but the traditionally prepared horseradish is lacto-fermented like sauerkraut. This makes for a very healthy probiotic condiment that will last for months in the refrigerator.

You might find it difficult to find fresh horseradish roots, but most well-stocked or ethnic grocery stores will have them, especially when in season.

Simple horseradish

This is the simplest of recipes and it's quick to prepare. While it won't feature the same deep flavor as the traditionally prepared and fermented horseradish, it's still very good.

<u>Yields about 1 ¾ cups</u>

Ingredients

1 cup peeled and minced horseradish root

3/4 cup white wine vinegar

1/4 tsp sea salt

Preparation

Process all the ingredients in a blender or food processor to a paste.

Enjoy right away or store in the refrigerator.

Beet Horseradish

This is a nice twist on the basic horseradish. In stores you will see this variation with bright red color.

Yields about 1 ¾ cups

Ingredients

3/4 lbs horseradish root, minced

1 cup finely chopped beets

3/4 cup apple cider vinegar

1/2 tsp sea salt

Preparation

Process all the ingredients in a blender or food processor to a paste.

Enjoy right away or store in the refrigerator.

Traditionally Fermented Horseradish

The recipe on the following page is for traditional horseradish requiring between 3 and 7 days of fermentation; but, it's a nice experiment to try with children and it will give you a wonderful and pungent probiotic condiment. You will also need a vegetable starter culture of some kind for the fermentation process to happen. Most health food stores will carry them, but you can also get a starter online at www.culturesforhealth.com. Caldwell and Body Ecology are good brands. These starters contain specific strains of bacteria that are especially suited for vegetable fermentation. You'll be able to use them for all your vegetable fermentation needs.

Fermented Horseradish Recipe

<u>Yields 1 cup</u>

Ingredients

1 cup horseradish, peeled & finely chopped

1 packet vegetable culture starter

2 Tbsp to 1/4 cup water

1 1/2 tsp sea salt

Preparation

In a food processor, combine the horseradish root, starter culture, sea salt and pulse to blend the ingredients.

Add about 3 Tbsp water and process again for about three minutes until the preparation takes the consistency of a paste. Add more water if necessary.

Place the horseradish paste in a small glass jar and add water on top to fill the jar.

Cover loosely with the lid and let stand in a warm place for between 3 and 7 days.

When ready, store in the refrigerator.

Worcestershire sauce

This sauce is traditionally a fermented sauce using anchovies, but the traditional recipe also calls for molasses and some hard to find ingredients. This simpler recipe contains perfectly healthy ingredients, apart from the bit of soy sauce used, which shouldn't be a problem in such a small quantity.

Yields 1 ¼ cup

Ingredients

1/2 cup apple cider vinegar

2 Tbsp water

2 Tbsp soy sauce

1/4 tsp ground ginger

1/4 tsp mustard powder

1/4 tsp onion powder

1/4 tsp garlic powder

1/8 tsp cinnamon

1/8 tsp freshly ground black pepper

Preparation

Combine all the ingredients in a saucepan and slowly bring to a bowl while stirring frequently. Let simmer for about a minute for the flavors to develop.

Cool and store in the refrigerator.

Barbecue Sauce

The BBQ sauce recipe on the following page will require more involvement than most of the other condiments because it calls for homemade mustard, ketchup and Worcestershire sauce. I think the best way to tackle it is to prepare BBQ sauce only when you already have those other condiments handy or if you decide to make a batch of all of those condiments all at once. It can become part of your weekly ritual to prepare some of the weekly Paleo food on a given day and to prepare some of the condiments at the same time.

This sauce has a nice smoky flavor, thanks to the smoked paprika, and will go well with your barbecued meat or simply as a side condiment with beef, pork or chicken. Unlike most barbecue sauces you'll find, this one doesn't use any sugar.

Barbecue Sauce

Yields 2 1/2 cups

Ingredients

1 onion, minced

1 clove garlic, minced

1 can (6 oz) tomato paste

1/2 cup apple cider vinegar

1/2 cup water

1/4 cup Paleo ketchup (see recipe on page 176 and 177)

3 Tbsp Paleo mustard (see page 179 and 181)

1 Tbsp Worcestershire sauce (recipe on page 191)

1 pinch ground cloves

1 pinch cinnamon

Smoked paprika to taste

Hot sauce to taste, optional (check the ingredients to make sure it's Paleo-friendly)

Preparation

In a large frying pan, with a bit of cooking fat, brown the onion for about 4 minutes.

Add the garlic and cook for another minute. Add all the other ingredients and simmer for 30 minutes.

Taste the sauce and adjust with more smoked paprika, vinegar or hot sauce to the desired taste. Cool and store in the refrigerator.

Meat Stock

I'm not all that precise when it comes to stock recipes. There isn't a need for precision and simple is always best. I make stock from everything. A really simple stock involves placing some bones in cold water with a tablespoon or two of cider vinegar and simmering on low until a rich stock evolves. For darker stock, roast your beef bones beforehand for 25 or 30 minutes at about 375 F.

Do not add salt to your stock. Especially if you plan to reduce it to make soups or sauces; the salt concentration will be too high. Only add salt in the end product in which you use the stock. Leave the fat in after it has cooked except for chicken stock where a good portion of the fat is polyunsaturated and will oxidize.

Experiment with your stocks. Mix things up and use bones from different animals all in the same pot.

How long does it take?

Allow around 4 hours for chicken stock and a minimum of 6 hours for other, tougher bones. You can easily let it go for much longer if you want to extract more taste and nutrients from the bones. I sometimes let it go for as much as 48 hours. I usually don't let it go for more than 24 hours for chicken stock since chicken bones are more fragile and after 24 hours there won't be much left. Just make sure you add water as it evaporates. You can make stock much faster in a pressure cooker taking as little as 40-60 minutes on high pressure.

Mirepoix, Bouquet Garni

A mirepoix is usually a mixture of diced carrots, celery and onions. The French use it in almost everything to flavor liquids because these vegetables impart such a great taste to the liquid. Add them only at the end if you're going for a 24 or 48-hour cooking period for the stock or else they'll disintegrate too much. They can be discarded afterwards because all the flavor and nutrients will be in the liquid.

A bouquet garni is a mixture of sturdy herbs like thyme, rosemary and bay leaves. They can be tied together, put in a pouch or simply placed in the liquid. You can also add fresh peppercorns for even more flavor.

After the cooking process

After your stock is cooked, it's a good idea to cool it fast or else bacteria will soon multiply in it. You can take the whole pot and put it in a sink filled with cold water. After it has been cooled, put what you want to use right away in the refrigerator and the rest in the freezer. It will keep for about a week in the refrigerator. Make sure it smells good and you should be fine.

To be sure it's sterile when you use it, bring it to a boil and cook for at least 10 minutes to make sure any bacteria is destroyed.

Paleo Fats

You've probably learned by now that good fats don't make you fat and that saturated fats are in the good fat category. In fact, fats make you happy, and for some of us Paleo dieters, it's our main source of energy. Our body is fully equipped to run primarily on fat as a source of energy.

Many of the recipes in this book use coconut fat because that's the cooking fat of choice for most Paleo dieters. But you can substitute any approved fat for the coconut fat in most recipes.

Don't get in a rut when choosing your fats. There is a broad variety of healthy fats to use; read on for ideas.

You should eliminate any vegetable oil high in polyunsaturated fatty acids and Omega-6. Examples of these oils include corn oil, peanut oil, soybean oil and grape seed oil.

Now for the good fats...

Coconut oil

This is a favorite fat in the Paleo world. In fact, practitioners of Paleo seek after all the products of the coconut, mainly because the list of benefits is so extensive.

Coconut oil is 92% saturated fat, which makes it really stable under heat and solid at room temperature. If you buy the virgin coconut oil, it will leave a great yet subtle coconut taste and smell to your dishes. The taste is something I like in almost any situation except maybe for eggs, where I prefer cooking with lard.

Coconut's main fatty acid content comes from lauric acid (47% to be precise). Lauric acid is a rare medium chain fatty acid, and is supposed to be the easiest fatty acid to digest. Lauric acid also has natural antimicrobial and antifungal properties.

Animal fats (Beef, duck, pork,...)

They are the essence of the reason we eat Paleo in the first place. Caveman ate animals—lots of them—for energy, therefore they obtained a lot of fat from animal sources.

Most animal fats are highly saturated and are therefore heat stable to cook at high temperatures. Conversely, they are solid at room temperature and don't need to be refrigerated. What's fun is that since they're not very popular because of their reputation, they're pretty cheap, even the ones coming from well-treated animals.

Just go to your butcher and ask for duck fat, pork lard or beef tallow. Your butcher might not have those fats rendered and ready for you to cook so you'll have to work a bit to use them, but you'll see it's nothing hard. Buy leaf lard or suet (beef).

Dry Method of Rendering Animal Fat

Remove any vein, meat or blood from the fat, and then chop it in very small chunks. Next, put the fat chunks either in a crock-pot or in a heavy-bottomed Dutch oven. Set the fat over very low heat. Once all the white fat chunks have become brown and dry, you can strain off the pure fat and let it cool. Be careful, as it will be very hot. Once cooled, it will be white and hard at room temperature. You are ready to cook with real animal fat!

Olive oil

Yes, it's a vegetable oil, but its content is mostly monounsaturated fat, a fat source that is safe and healthy. Don't cook with it, it will burn and oxidize quite easily. Use it in dressings or put on top of your already cooked meals. As you probably know, a good extra-virgin olive oil offers many great health benefits.

Fresh oils in dark bottles that haven't been on the shelf for a long time are the best. Keep in a dark and cool place to increase shelf life. You can store it in the fridge if not using promptly. It will become cloudy in the refrigerator, but will return to normal once back at room temperature.

Avocados and avocado oil

Avocado is a fruit, one of the only fatty fruits. It contains a lot of vitamin E, B vitamins, potassium and fiber. Its fat content is mostly monounsaturated, so it's a good fat choice. It's not particularly heat stable though, so don't cook at high temperature with it. Instead, use avocado oil for your salad dressings. Also, sliced avocados are delicious with salads, chicken or as guacamole (recipe on page 171) with lemon juice and tomatoes.

Of course there are other sources of fat you can consume like eggs, nuts and nut butters. I would be careful with nuts and nut butters though because most nuts are very high in Omega-6, which could trigger inflammation and other digestive problems. Try out several different oils and go with what feels and tastes right for you.

Exercise and Paleo

By Dustin Mohr

Dustin Mohr owns and operates "Mohr Fitness" in Johnson City, Tennessee. Dustin is an East Tennessee State University graduate and former collegiate athlete. Dustin has helped thousands in the Tri-Cities area reach their fitness goals through the Paleo Diet and Crossfit style exercise. He is certified through Expert Rating Global Certifications. Mohr Fitness endorses the Crossfit philosophy, but is not an affiliate.

Over the past decade, I have seen hundreds of diets and exercise routines come and go. The diets generally last for several weeks, focusing on a very fast and intense fat loss phase. The exercise routines are usually one to two months in duration, with each day mapped out ahead of time.

Sometimes, I even see a workout plan with a diet to go along with it. These are usually pretty decent programs. However, in these fitness magazines and websites, we see a different exercise program and a different diet every single month. Why is that? It's because these diet and exercise programs are focused on how much attention they can grab in a short period of time. The routines must be new, the movements must be flashy, and a new one must be introduced every month to keep the reader excited and entertained. The reason we see a different diet and exercise program every month, is because they are <u>fads</u>, not lifestyles. In my experience, the only true partnership of diet and exercise that is sustainable, effective, and doesn't change every month is the combination of the Paleo Diet with Crossfit style exercise.

I own and operate a gym with a similar philosophy to that of the Crossfit franchise. The Crossfit community has really got things figured out as far as fitness goes. The approach is simple, easy to understand, and effective for the most elite young athlete to the feeblest elderly person. The name Crossfit insinuates the definition of fitness for the franchise, which is to be fit across a multitude of standards. So, by Crossfit standards, marathon runners are not the fittest people on earth, because they most certainly lack strength and muscle mass.

On the other hand, elite power lifters and body builders are not the fittest people on earth either, because they most certainly lack endurance and flexibility. So, a person who is "Cross fit" isn't the fastest runner in the world, or the strongest person in the world, but rather a person who has balance in every area of fitness. The other area that the Crossfit community has figured out is the focus on movement rather than muscles. In most fitness magazines you will read, the exercises focus on certain body parts and working them specifically. Crossfit focuses on movements such as pushing, pulling, squatting, running, jumping, throwing, etc. Training with these movements that humans have performed for years and continue to perform on a daily basis has become known as "functional training". So rather than making a muscle bigger and aesthetically pleasing with no purpose or function, Crossfitters focus on how to enhance the performance and functionality of all the muscles involved, and know that the growth and appearance will follow.

So what does a Crossfit workout look like? There are a multitude of movements associated with Crossfit, ranging from weightlifting, to bodyweight movements such as pull-ups and pushups, to metabolic conditioning such as running and swimming. The reason there isn't a different Crossfit routine in "Shape Magazine" every month is that the movements are combined in as many different patterns as possible. So, the routine is that there is no routine! Routine is the enemy, and with a different workout in store every day, it's impossible to plateau or become bored. The duration of Crossfit workouts also differ significantly from those of mainstream fitness magazines. All Crossfit workouts are short and intense, averaging between 15 and 30 minutes in duration. With a combination of all of these movements in an all-out burst of effort, the need to perform weight training and cardiovascular work separately is eliminated. All of your muscle building and fat loss efforts can be attained in one short workout. These anaerobic workouts are more effective than hours of aerobic work for fat loss. The answer lies in the effect of intense, anaerobic, total body training on the body's metabolism.

When a human being performs aerobic exercise, he or she burns the maximum amount of calories in the "fat burning zone". However, as soon as he or she stops exercising, the body returns to its normal metabolic rate within minutes. So, the number of calories the person burns is how many were burned from the exercise, period. When a person performs an intense, total body, anaerobic workout, his or her heart rate and metabolism are elevated to such a high level that the body's metabolic rate will not return to normal for hours, or even days. For this reason, Crossfit style workouts burn calories not only during the workout, but also for hours after. This is the magic of the fat loss effect in these workouts.

It seems so simple, that focusing on things that humans have done for years could be the most effective style of exercise in existence. This is exactly the same approach the Paleo Diet takes; eliminating unnecessary, useless ideas, and focusing on real, time-tested things that work for a broad range of people. For this reason, those who combine the Paleo Diet lifestyle with the Crossfit lifestyle are among the strongest, leanest, healthiest people alive. For more information on this style of exercise and its integration with the Paleo Diet, visit my website www.getmohrfit.com and check out www.crossfit.com.

Make your own Meal Plan Template

Day	Week 1	Week 2
Mon	B: L: D:	B: L: D:
Tue	B: L: D:	B: L: D:
Wed	B: L: D:	B: L: D:
Thu	B: L: D:	B: L: D:
Fri	B: L: D:	B: L: D:
Sat	B: L: D:	B: L: D:
Sun	B: L: D:	B: L: D:

Make your own Meal Plan Template

Day	Week 3	Week 4
Mon	B: L: D:	B: L: D:
Tue	B: L: D:	B: L: D:
Wed	B: L: D:	B: L: D:
Thu	B: L: D:	B: L: D:
Fri	B: L: D:	B: L: D:
Sat	B: L: D:	B: L: D:
Sun	B: L: D:	B: L: D:

Make your own Meal Plan Template

Day	Week 1	Week 2
Mon	B: L: D:	B: L: D:
Tue	B: L: D:	B: L: D:
Wed	B: L: D:	B: L: D:
Thu	B: L: D:	B: L: D:
Fri	B: L: D:	B: L: D:
Sat	B: L: D:	B: L: D:
Sun	B: L: D:	B: L: D:

Make your own Meal Plan Template

Day	Week 1	Week 2
Mon	B: L: D:	B: L: D:
Tue	B: L: D:	B: L: D:
Wed	B: L: D:	B: L: D:
Thu	B: L: D:	B: L: D:
Fri	B: L: D:	B: L: D:
Sat	B: L: D:	B: L: D:
Sun	B: L: D:	B: L: D:

Your Notes:

1626112R00115

Printed in Germany
by Amazon Distribution
GmbH, Leipzig